THE ADVENT OF CHRIST

OTHER TITLES:

THE GOSPEL OF JOHN BY JAKOB LORBER
(6 volumes = 2,113 pg.)

This monumental work reveals never-known insights regarding all questions pertaining to God, creation, the reason for living and eternity.

SUNSET INTO SUNRISES BY JAKOB LORBER
(487 pg.)

Among the writings about "life after death", this book ranks very high.

JESUS' WORDS BY JAKOB LORBER
(176 pg.)

A collection of the Words of Jesus from the works of Jakob Lorber.

GEMS OF THE MASTER OF ALL MASTERS BY JAKOB LORBER & WALTER FLOREANI
(108 pg.)

A beautiful selection of the Lord's Words which will give inspiration to contemplation and reflections, with photographs by Walter Floreani.

A SPIRITUAL VIEW OF LIFE BY JAKOB LORBER & GOTTFRIED MAYERHOFER
(236 pg.)

This book reveals from a spiritual point-of-view, the spiritual anatomy of man, the spiritual vision of the universe, light and sound - spiritual elements and the essence of the natural order.

FUNDAMENTAL PRINCIPLES OF LIFE BY WALTER LUTZ
(3 volumes = 1,064 pg.)

The content is taken from the wealth of the messages of Jakob Lorber regarding the most important questions of life.

THE LORD'S SERMONS BY GOTTFRIED MAYERHOFER
(326 pg.)

This book contains 53 sermons for every Sunday of the traditional church year. A quote from the epilogue: "These sermons should be like steps which gradually should teach you to know Me, My Teachings and yourself better, and expand your insights."

THE ADVENT OF CHRIST

A Portrayal of Mankind's Development

Excerpts from the Revelations

Received through the Inner Word

By

Jakob Lorber

and

Gottfried Mayerhofer

Merkur Publishing Co. Ltd., Canada

©Lorber-Verlag, 712 Bietigheim, West Germany

Originally translated from the German by Violet Ozols and Hedwig Groll

All rights in this book are reserved. No part of this book may be reproduced in any form without written permission from the publisher except for brief quotation embodied in critical articles for reviews.

Published by Merkur Publishing Co. Ltd., Canada
Under License

ISBN 09693820-6-5

Second Edition 1992 Edited by Gerhard Hanswille

Printed in the United States of America

CONTENTS

Preface vii

The Great Dawn Preceding the Coming of the Lord 9

The Personal Advent of the Lord 18

A Portrayal of Mankind's Development 35

Biblical Interpretations 42

The "Antichrist" 48

The Present Spiritual Deluge 50

The Powers of Heaven will be Shaken 52

The Thousand-Year Kingdom (the Millennium) 53

The Sevenfold Coming of the Lord 55

The Great and New Jerusalem 56

Interpretation of the Second Chapter of Isaiah 59

Explanation of the Future Metaphors of Isaiah 62

Exegesis of Isaiah 2:6-22 64

Exegesis of the Third Chapter of Isaiah 67

The Collapse of the False Religious Framework 71

The Number 666 74

The Revelation of John 75

Explanation of the Revelation of John 77

PREFACE

Earlier editions of this work by Jakob Lorber (1800-1864) and Gottfried Mayerhofer (1807-1877) were published under the title "The Great Advent". However, we are now no longer at the beginning of the season of The Great Advent in expectation of the immense change of mankind from the physical to the spirit. We are already in the midst of the twilight of the dawning which must precede the rising of the new sun of the spirit. The chaos in our present days cannot deceive us where all the gloomy mists violently begin to brew. At this point, it would be more appropriate to speak of The Return of Christ, rather than The Great Advent.

The more distinct the contrast between light and darkness, the more definite the separation of the spirits within all of humanity is executed; and all the signs of the times pointing clearly to a very close, last and final battle where the will for good or evil will decisively face each other. Only a great awakening of mankind will be able to bring about the victory of the Divine Spirit above everything that is demonic and an enemy of life. And, because of freedom of will, the demonic forces will be allowed to increase only once more, and as a consequence of this increase, they will lose all of their power.

The great prophecies of Jesus are conveyed through the inner word, as received by Jakob Lorber and also by Gottfried Mayerhofer, and form the content of this book. There will be no doubt in the mind of the enlightened reader as to final victory of the spirit over the anti-spirit, and this alone will be able to provide such inner tranquillity which will liberate the people of today from their great world fear. As a result of this, they will face, full of trust, the Coming Events. Every worldly last judgment, as a consequence of human disregard of God's Laws, will be changed through Divine Love into Blissfulness.

Not the downfall of the world, but a great purification of mankind will and must precede the "Coming of Christ in the Human Spirit", and the Word of the Revelation of John of a "new earth" and a "new heaven" will be fulfilled. Whosoever will faithfully accept into his heart the here newly-presented prophetic words about our end times, will gain with them entrance into a spiritual ark, that will carry them into a new time over and above all rising floods of coming events in nature and in the world. This will be the countenance of the spiritual Advent of Christ imprinted with all its delightful, blissful adherence to His Teachings.

May these writings give light, strength and recognition in the sense of the Great Events in the midst of which we are presently standing.

The Editor

THE GREAT DAWN PRECEDING THE COMING OF THE LORD

(Received through Jakob Lorber in 1849)

Whosoever has a light, let him not place it under a covered table where it would be shining in vain. But whosoever is endowed with some light, let him place his little lamp upon the table where it may burn and light up the table and the chamber. If, in this manner, many little lights are brightly shining from the table, it becomes so bright that every guest entering the room will say in wonder: "Why is it so bright here! How enjoyable this is to our well-being after having walked through the long night! Indeed, it comes to us like a scarlet dawn!"

"Light invigorates life and truly awakens it even if only produced artificially, i.e. by way of pure reason and a purified intellect. Hence, it is necessary that in these times, everyone who is in possession of a good and useful little lamp - bring it forth. Let him clean it properly, fill it with plenty of oil, light it and then put it upon the table of purer recognition, where it may give light to those around the table or those present in the chamber.

The course of events in these days clearly show what is mostly lacking, namely the light. Therefore, what is the use of talking about love or the observance of God's Commandments, if those to whom the sermon is preached are in utter darkness! Would they not bluntly tell the preachers: 'What do you prattle, disciples of the night, trying to make me believe things you have neither seen nor experienced? If you put a light on the table and describe in detail what you see and notice, I shall be able to believe you, for the light from your lamp will also illuminate my little chamber! Hence, before you preach to us, ignite a light yourself; then we shall believe what you are now trying to make us believe in the total darkness of night.'"

"Therefore, it is not only spoken of to those who have good will and those who are in need of the teachings of true life, but it is also addressed to all teachers: Once the little lamps are well-supplied with oil, they shall be lit without delay and placed upon the hospitable table of true insight and recognition. For the day has approached when the last great promise will be fulfilled! It is written how this time will be. And behold, the predicted signs are all here. Who could fail to recognize them?

But should the prophesied events have already occurred unequivocally, who would continue to doubt any further the fact that soon The Great Day will be here? The Great Day which will mark the coming-again of the Lord and thusly the unending Advent of the Lord! Did not the two angels from the heavens say to those who lamented over the Lord's loss at the place where He ascended into His Kingdom: 'Why do you remain here with so much sorrow, gazing after the One who has ascended into His Kingdom? Go home in peace, for this Jesus, whom you have now seen ascending into the heaven of all heavens, will once again, as He has ascended now, descend again to judge the generations on earth. Blessed are they whom He will find righteous; they shall become His Children and He their Lord and Father! But woe betide those who have remained unrighteous; truly, their responsibility is sure to become a millstone around their neck!'"

"What these two angels of God and what I, as the Lord and God Himself, have prophesied concerning the future Advent of Christ, has now come to maturity and will soon take place. Almost all of the necessary preparations have been set into motion. Men's hearts are now reflecting these times with their horrible manifestations. They are possessed of tyranny, miserliness, envy, gluttony, fornication, strife, discord, slander, robbery, war, murder, and pestilence of every kind. Discord, unkindness and unmercifulness have taken possession of them and through this, a misery has come over humanity as never before experienced on earth. Therefore, this miserable time must soon be ended, otherwise even the up-to-now Chosen Ones could suffer isolation.

However, before I, as the Lord and Creator of all life can return, the earth must be completely cleansed of all weeds; and this is now taking place in all parts of the earth. Whosoever now has a wilfully sick soul and does not endeavour to get his soul healed, will not have much time left before he perishes.

The shortest period of purification will be four weeks because from now on there will be hours where more things will happen than in one century of the past. A longer period of four months has been set, for there will be periods where there will be days which will be more significant than formerly a full century. Still a further time has been set for four quarters of a year, for during one week more will be happening than formerly during a full century. And the longest time has been set for four years and a little bit more, for there will now be months during which more will be happening than formerly during seven centuries!

This time, however, is now like a scarlet dawn preceding that day which will come as a salvation for the righteous and for all of those with a good and gentle heart who love their brothers and sisters in My Name. But this day will also come like a thief over all those who disregard Me, have a hard and proud heart and regard themselves as better, and who hold themselves in higher esteem than their brothers.

Whosoever regards himself in any way whatsoever as better than his brother will, on this day be ruined, for from this day on, all external differences will cease to exist. Those who now, for the sake of My Name are despised, or just out of pity tolerated as honest people, will be greatly honoured. On this day, such people will go forth as great and glorious, whereas those who are now so very ambitious, will become quite insignificant. But My Elect will be shining brighter than the sun at noon!

A natural, scarlet dawn does not announce a beautiful day. There is an old proverb which states: The morning redness becomes the day's predicament and causes the evening's death. But with the spiritual, scarlet dawn the opposite is the case. Whilst a natural, rosy dawn invigorates all hearts, the spiritual dawn will fill them with great fear and anxiety, for it will derive its color from the blood and the great blaze of the world, by which the great and small wars are to be understood.

As the natural, scarlet dawn is an unfavourable sign for the break of day, the as-such unpleasant spiritual dawn can be regarded as a most favourable forerunner for The Coming Great Day of Salvation. This is the way I arranged it, and I shall allow things to take their course.

Whosoever will dare to cross My Path and say to Me: 'Lord, You are a cruel God; the blood of the slaughtered gives You pleasure and You act like an eternal tyrant!' Let Me tell him: The reason for the Master's existence is not to be judged by His works or deeds, but He will judge them in a just and righteous manner. Therefore, you shall also not say: 'Behold, this nation is in the right and that one is unjust, or this or the other general acts in a more damnable way than his predecessors.' Nor should you have joy or sorrow if one or the other party has gained a victory or has been conquered. Altogether, you must not be too much concerned with the things that now happen, whether they are right or wrong. For I permit all of this to happen in this way, and I am Lord enough to be wise and good! But if someone believes himself to be wiser, let him master the elements, show the stars their course and command the winds, the sea, and the mighty fire in the inner earth!

I tell you: Do not interfere in anything, but stay at home, so when I come soon, I may find you at home, strengthen you and receive you into My newly to-be-established Kingdom on earth and in all the stars! However, if I do not find you at home, you can only blame yourself if you do not at all, or only in a very limited way, participate in My Greatest and Final Advent.

Actually, there is before Me fundamentally only one sin which is the mother of all others and it is called: Pride! Out of pride comes forth everything else that is sin, like selfishness, lust for power, self-love, envy, avarice, usury, deceit, thievery, robbery, anger, murder, laziness, idleness, and a propensity for a life of pleasure; also boasting, lewdness of the flesh, unchastity, harlotry and, finally, forgetting God. Often also complete godlessness and with it total disobedience of all the laws of divine origin. If you look at each of these archsins, you will find pride at its root. Therefore, if someone would like to eliminate all of his presumed many sins with one stroke, let him make every effort to free himself of any kind of pride. Sins that are committed without pride are not really sins because they do not contain within them the basis for sin.

Let everyone allow this scarlet dawn to shine through him thoroughly, and let him carefully search in all corners of his life to see if he may not find something resembling pride. If he encounters something in his innermost like pride, then he should immediately strive with all of his powers to eliminate his pride, even if it appears to be insignificant. Or, with time, this will gradually grow and ruin the otherwise noble human being spiritually, just as a parasite would an otherwise completely healthy tree. Pride, in any form whatsoever is, for the soul and the spirit, a highly poisonous, suffocating air from hell through which all life must perish in no time.

Therefore, I repeat: Beware of pride above all if you want to appear justified before Me and enjoy My visible presence on The Coming Great Day! But as long as only an atom of pride still remains within you, I shall not come to you because you did not renounce this basic evil, even though you know what millions only hazard to guess. But that does not make you in the least any better than those who have no knowledge of the things that with you has already become experienced knowledge, sometimes even virtual vision. However, the profound knowledge in the sphere of the purely spiritual will be of immeasurable benefit to you only if your knowledge is also combined with the right humility.

I tell you: Do not seek the honour of the world in whatever form! It is a pestilence for the soul and spirit and, sooner or later, its devastating consequences will become apparent. Look at the wars where for the sake of honour millions were slain. If rulers, commanders-in-chief and their nations, were to serve celestial humility instead of pride, could the nations ever be inflamed with such fury towards each other? Indeed, with humble nations a war would be an impossibility. However, since with all the nations pride has grown tall, causing one nation to consider itself better, more distinguished, older and with greater rights than the other, the all-devastating wars are a natural consequence of the breeding of pride.

It would be an entirely different matter if a greedy or spiteful enemy, in order to plunder, invaded a peaceful country inhabited by a humble and most peaceable people. Then, of course, the inhabitants of such a country would have the right to receive and punish such an infamous enemy with all severity, in which case I, as the Lord, would promptly take the lead. The evil enemy would then very soon experience what reward his actions merited, and would hardly ever again have the courage to overrun such a land. Unfortunately, it is not so. One nation wants to be greater than the other, one kingdom mightier than the next.

The arrogance of the nations has gone too far. The vapour of hell has already risen to the highest heaven! Earth itself prayed to Me to finally eliminate the evil brood of Satan! And behold, the time has come, revealed before your eyes: One nation wages war against the other! If you ask why, I tell you: purely out of pride! I also tell you: The times are past when the sword would act as arbiter between honour and shame, virtue and vice. For the sword has never been a weapon of humility, but always of honour and self-importance, and only too often also of tyranny.

It will no longer be so! In the future, humility will be ruling the nations with weapons of love. This will, of course, apply only to those nations that will be found worthy of this weapon from the heavens. In these times, the unworthy will receive their long-deserved rewards. I will always give victory to the better and more righteous party; but should that one then become arrogant, woe betide him, too!

From now on, no one shall be spared who, in his actions, has even a spark of pride as a motivation. Every action that shows any ambition shall, from now on, remain without a blessing, whereas every action performed with a humble heart for the sake of usefulness shall be richly blessed by Me. Now a different order has to be introduced among men. But those who will not submit with all their hearts to this order, and still allow their former traditions to emerge within them before obtaining enough information, shall soon be shown by the most bitter consequences whether they were acting for or against My Order."

"I am telling you at this time: Whosoever, because of the world, will fail to do one or the other good deed, let him act for the sake of the world in the way he deems to be good. But when he will then come to Me with a good worldly testimonial, I shall say to him: Go to the one who gave you this good testimonial and ask for your reward; for My Name is not written on this testimonial! For the sake of the world you have done this or that, and did not want to walk the only path of true humility pleasing to Me. It flattered your ambition when the world said of you: 'Behold, that is a man of honour!' Then it must also please you that in My Kingdom, you will truly only come to minor honours. With this I do not mean to say that a person is to act in a way that the world will point at him with contempt. Oh no, I do not ever demand that! But I do demand that you accomplish what is truly good - may the world say to it whatever it wants - without any bashfulness whatsoever. And that is because it is good and I want it that way.

Have you forgotten that I, as the arch-eternal, almighty Creator of all the heavens and worlds, angels and men, have Myself come into the world, clothed only in the greatest humbleness? I taught men through living words and clearest deeds that they like Me - if they want to be My Children - shall flee the world with its greatness and magnificence and not walk the wide road of earthly splendour, which is always perishable, but walk the narrow path of humility which leads to the Eternal Life.

And that besides, everything that is great before the world is an abomination before Me? That I regard only the small things, despised by the world and reject forever that which imagines itself to be great?

You shall not view My Countenance until the last atom of pride has been eliminated from your heart. Verily, this is how it will be! Every sinner shall be treated by Me with more leniency than one who has not banned, with true repentance and deep abhorrence, his obvious pride from his heart forever! If you had as many sins as there is grass on the earth and sand on the shores of the sea, but showed no trace of any pride, all these sins would be as if they were nothing before Me! *For where there is no pride, there is love which contains all humility within it.* Love and humility obliterates all faults and sins, be there ever so many. However, if there is just an atom of pride behind all the other sins people commit during the probation time of their becoming free, this atom will stimulate all sins, even the smallest. Such spirits will have in the future, as they do in the present, a mighty struggle to dispose themselves of even an atom of pride.

Mere atoms of pride are sufficient to make it impossible for Me to enter the innermost of otherwise quite worthy human beings until the last atom of it will have left their hearts. This is the reason why, especially in these times, so few people get to see Me and are taught by Me personally, and can be reared to be My Children.

Do also no longer say: 'This house, this ground and this property belong to me. I am the master in my house and have to work my own land!' Behold, there is quite a great portion of pride hidden in such remarks! Verily, I shall never come to those who think, speak and act like this, because they do not regard Me as the Lord Who truly owns everything, but only themselves as lords over things I have lent them but for a short time. Therein lies an immense amount of pride - the sole producer of all wars, whether on a large or a small scale. In My Future Kingdom this will be arranged in a considerably different way. There will no longer be any landlords and land barons, for there I will be the All-in-All. And he with whom I shall take up residence will be in the best position!

However, mind this: Before My Advent upon this earth, many of the weeds and much dry grass will be exterminated with a judgment of great severity. Wherever there are two, one will be accepted and the other one rejected; thus there will be a great sifting out of more than one-half! Once more I warn you in all earnest that in these times you do not sway either right or left! Who shall be victorious is solely in My Hand! Let none of you say: This one is right in his fight, that one is wrong, but it is your duty to pray for friend and foe. What is beyond that is sin, for through taking sides, you draw unto yourselves the pride of the party which you wish to be victorious, thereby wishing complete downfall of the opposition. But do ask your heart whether those who were to perish are not your brothers, just as those to whom you wish victory?'

How is such a wish, full of secret vengefulness and

gloating, consistent with My Word? Did not I Myself teach all human beings to pray for those who hate you, to bless those that curse you, and to do good unto them that wish you evil? Therefore, let them fight who are fighting! Pray for all, and never take delight in the defeat of others; then you will be like My angels in heaven who cover their countenance when their brothers on earth kill each other.

Take note of this: The scarlet dawn preceding My Advent will still become much redder than it already is. And only at the end of all destruction will it become clear that neither one nor the other fighting party will have gained an actual victory, for the true victor is yet to come. Where now pride is fighting, humility will begin to fight and no ruthless tyrant will escape its sword nor a judge who endeavoured to establish his authority through the blood of harmless prisoners.

I, as your eternal Father, who has already given you so much, am now giving you this most important word for your future welfare and salvation. Keep it faithfully and strictly, then you will find all blessings temporally and eternally. However, if you regard it only as something common and continue with your old habits and customs, you will have only yourselves to blame if you have very little or no part at all in My Advent.

What has been written here through My servant will be fulfilled irrevocably. Blessed are you and everyone who will not disregard these warnings; his house I will surely visit now and then!

But whosoever will not pay much attention to this admonition and similar advice given in many instances, nor be of good will and lend an ear - his house will be desolate, deplorable, and deserted. For when I come, I shall come only to those who are truly My Own and I will personally bless them over and over eternally!

Woe betide him in whose entrance hall I shall not be setting foot; his share will be and will remain the sad and ominous scarlet dawn and the holy rays of The Coming Great Day will not fall upon him! This say I Who will be coming. Amen."

THE PERSONAL ADVENT OF THE LORD

Excerpt from the messages received through Jakob Lorber, about the teachings and acts of Jesus during the time of His ministry. Taken from the Great Gospel of John, where the Lord spoke to His disciples on this subject as follows:

1.

Received through Jakob Lorber -
"I showed them how the furtive prince of the world will soon have to face his judgment and soon after that, also his cohorts. At the same time I showed them the end of the world[1] and a universal judgment similar to the one at the time of Noah. Amazed, they asked Me when and how this would happen. But I told them: As it was at the time of Noah, it will be then, too: Love will wane and completely grow cold. Belief in a pure life precept and recognition of God, as revealed to mankind from the heavens, will be changed to dark, dead superstition, full of falsehood and deceit. The ruling power will again make use of human beings like animals and have them killed cold-bloodedly and without conscience if they do not submit to their will without protest."

"The ruling power will plague the poor with all kinds of pressure and will persecute and suppress every free spirit with all available means. Through these deeds, mankind will be subjected to such tribulations as never before experienced on planet earth. But then, because of the many Chosen Ones who will be found among the poor, the days will be shortened. For if this did not happen, even the Chosen Ones could perish! Until that time, however, another one-thousand years, and not quite another one-thousand years will pass! - Then I will send

---

[1] In this instance, "end of the world" does not mean that the earth will perish. Instead it means the cessation of the preponderance of materialism and its reign, such as egoism, lust for power, and hence the beginning of acknowledged spirituality, i.e. a positive, spiritual life philosophy as is ideally given in the pure Teachings of Jesus, His Life and activities. (The Ed.)

the same angels you now see here[2] with great trumpets among the poor. These angels will awaken the spiritually dead human beings of the earth from the graves of their night. And these many millions of awakened will then, rolling like a column of fire from one end of the world to the other, overthrow the world powers, and no one will be able to resist them!"

"From then on, the earth will once more become a paradise and I will forever be leading My Children onto the right path. However, from then on, after one-thousand years have passed, the prince of darkness will once more, for a short period of seven years and several months and days, be free for his own sake, either for his total fall or a possible return. In the first instance, the inner part of the earth will be transformed into an eternal prison whereas the outer earth will remain a paradise.

In the second instance, however, earth would be changed into heaven, and the death of the flesh and the soul would cease forever! - How will this happen, and when? Not even the first angel of heaven is allowed to know in advance when that will occur. Only the Father alone knows!..."

"There will be a time when there are many human beings who only seek the pleasures on earth; God will soon allow a universal world judgment over all of mankind to take place. Then we shall see whether following that there will still be people who, with a measuring rule in their hand, will dare say to their fellowman: 'Look, I have measured this great tract of land, have placed the boundary stones in position and declare it as my own incontestable property.' And if anyone should dare to contest it or just say: 'Friend, everyone has the same right, provided he has the power and the means to wrench your imagined right out of your hands; such a human being I will sentence to death!' - I tell you: Such a person will no longer exist! For when I shall again come to this earth to pass judgment over such 'epicureans', but also to hand the reward

---

[2]Angels were visibly present i.e. in perfect human form - materialized perfected, highest spirits; for instance, Gabriel, Raphael, Zuriel and others (See John 1:51): "Verily, I say unto you, hereafter ye shall see heaven open and the angels of God ascending and descending upon the Son of Man". (The Ed.)

of life to everyone who out of love for God and his neighbour has suffered much misery and distress, - then the land shall not be measured for somebody's sole benefit. Wherever one will be, he will be able to harvest and satisfy his needs. And people will be helping each other, but no one will say: 'Look, this is my property over which I am lord!'

Then mankind will realize that I alone am the Lord, but that all of them are brothers and sisters. It should also be this way among mankind now. However, in this intermediate development period for mankind, those who have not yet been purified through the great fire of life, are allowed to remain as they are, but not for a full two-thousand years from now. Following this, the spirit of mankind will gain a great preponderance, and there will no longer be any measured "mine" and "thine" on planet earth. From God's point of view, the entire earth belongs to all people equally, as was the case in the beginning. The sages were to divide it in accordance with people's needs and teach them to cultivate the soil. The fruits were then to be partly distributed by the wise men and the surplus stored in specially erected storehouses, so that no one in the community should suffer want..."

"The fire preceding My Advent will be called: The great and universal plight, misery and tribulation as never before seen on earth. Faith will cease to exist, love will grow cold and all the poor people will lament and starve. The great and mighty, however, and the kings of this world will not help the supplicants, due to their great arrogance and hardness of heart Then one nation will rise against another and will wage war with firearms. Through this, the rulers will get into debt and will torment their subjects with excessive taxes. The result will be a very high cost of living, famine, many serious diseases, epidemics and pestilence among human beings, animals and even plants. There will also be great storms on land and sea, as well as earthquakes. The sea will flood its shores in many places and people will suffer great anxiety and will live in great fear and anticipation of the things to come on planet earth! All this will be allowed to happen in order to turn people away from their pride, egoism and indolence. Behold, that is *the first gradation of fire* through which mankind will be purified for My Coming Advent.

At the same time, also the natural fire will have to perform a mighty service: The fire will be driving the ships on all the seas with the speed of the winds. Thanks to their keen intellect, mankind will be making iron waggons and roads; and instead of having animals pull the waggons, they will be employing fire and with its power, they will travel the earth with the speed of an arrow. They will also know how to control the flash of lightning (electricity) and make it the fastest conveyor of their will from one end of the earth to the other. And when the proud and greedy kings wage war against each other, the fire will be the deciding factor. For through its force, very heavy, spherical iron masses will be hurled with lightning speed, against the enemy, against cities and fortresses, causing great devastation. With these weapons, ingenious mankind will arrive at a point where no nation will be able to start a war against another, for if two nations should attack each other with such weapons, they would soon destroy one another to the last man, which would surely give none of them a true victory or be of benefit. The kings and commanders will soon realize this and will, therefore, rather live in peace and friendship. And in case a particularly arrogant and ambitious troublemaker should arise and wage war against his neighbour, the peaceable ones would unite and punish him. In this manner, gradually, the former peace will return to the nations on earth and become permanent. There will still be wars among the more primitive people, but even among those nations war will soon become an impossibility. Through my righteous kings and commanders, I will have the nations of the world paired off and I will pour out My Light among them, and they will be changed into peaceful and light-friendly nations. Behold, this is *the second gradation of fire* through which mankind will be purified!

The third gradation of fire will consist in that I shall, already a few hundred years earlier, awaken ever more enlightened seers, prophets and servants (e.g. the reformers, Boehme, Swedenborg and now 'the new light'; in addition, also the light of science. Ed.) who will teach the nations everywhere the truth in My Name.

Thereby they will deliver them from all kinds of delusions, deceit and falsehood which through the false prophets and priests who, even in My Name, will be paving the way for their downfall. The false prophets and priests will, in a very short time, herewith commence their evil beginnings which here and there already began in My Time. These false prophets will be working false signs and miracles, like the pagan priests. They will seduce many human beings, thereby gaining great earthly treasures and riches, power and respect. But through the third fire and its brightest light, they will lose everything and be ruined. The kings and princes willing to help them will be losing all their power, their wealth and their thrones. For I shall awaken My Own kings and commanders who will defeat them, and thus the former night of hell and its messengers on earth among men will come to an end. Through *the third gradation of fire* from the heavens will falsehood be defeated in its fight with the light of truth, just as natural night must succumb before the rising sun! It must flee into its dark caves and depths; and once a person is in the light, he will no longer seek the night.

And now I will show you also *a fourth gradation of fire* through which the earth, mankind and my whole creation will be purified at the time of My Second Coming. This kind of fire will consist in all kinds and generations of great natural cataclysms, especially in those places on earth where mankind will have built too large and too magnificent cities. There will be present and ruling the greatest of pride, lovelessness, corruption, false courts of justice, might, authority, indolence and at the same time extreme poverty and all kinds of troubles and misery, brought about by the boundless pleasure-seeking and indulgence of the high and mighty. Also, in those cities a variety of factories will be established on a large scale in which, instead of human hands, fire and water combined with thousands of ingenious machines made from iron will be doing the work. For the firing, the very old earth-coal will be used which the people of that time will be procuring from the depths of the earth in very large quantities.

When this activity will, through the power of fire, have reached its peak, the earth's atmosphere will in such spots be saturated with the combustible types of ether which will then ignite at one point here and at another point there, and will reduce cities and regions into ruins and ashes, together with many of the inhabitants. That will then be a great and effective purification, too! However, what this type of fire will not be able to accomplish, will be achieved by all kinds of great storms. This will, of course, happen only where it is needed, for without necessity nothing will be burnt or destroyed. Through this, the earth's atmosphere will also be liberated of its harmful vapours and evil nature-spirits, and this will have a beneficial influence on all other creatures on earth. It will also serve humanity's physical health in that all the numerous and evil diseases of their bodies will cease and people will be able to reach a ripe, old age in health and in strength.

Since the thus-purified people will be standing alive in My Light and at all times actively and truly observe the Commandments of Love, all earthly property will be distributed among mankind in such a way that everyone will have enough, so that with proper diligence no one will ever suffer need. The heads of communities and the kings standing in My Light will be totally under My Will, and they will see to it that there is never any need among the people in their land. And I Myself will be visiting people everywhere, strengthening and comforting them, wherever I shall find the greatest yearning and the greatest love for Me. This prophecy, of course, concerns a time in the still distant future, but it will be fulfilled. For everything can pass away, even this earth and the entire visible firmament, but not My Words and promises every one of which will be fulfilled!

At that time there will be many new places, lands and nations which at present have no name. However, you can be assured that I shall come again to the earth only in such a place where, among human beings, the greatest and most-alive faith and the greatest and truest love towards God and their fellowman exists. And when I come again, I shall not be coming alone, but all My Own, those who will have been with Me in My heavens, will accompany Me in great numbers and strengthen their brothers who are still walking in the flesh on earth. Thus, there will be a true communion between the already most-blessed spirits of the heavens and human beings of this earth, which is certain to be the greatest comfort to the people of that time. And now you know all you need know. Act accordingly and you will gain Eternal Life, for I will awaken you on Judgement Day!"

"I cannot tell you the year, the day or the hour of My Coming, because everything on this earth depends on the absolute free will of mankind. Therefore, no angel in heaven knows this either; only the Father knows, and He will reveal it only to those of His choosing. Besides, having this particular prior knowledge does not necessarily serve the salvation of the soul. It is only for those few who are totally reborn in the spirit, but for countless others it would be a great evil! Therefore, it is better for mankind not to know everything in advance as to what, how and when in this world one or the other thing can overcome him or must happen to him. I tell you: A time will be coming when you (in the descendants of your faith) will ask, as you are doing now, when the day of the Son of Man will come? They will desire to see Him and still not see Him in accordance to their desire. In those times many will arise and say with a wise mien: Look here, look there, and that is the day! But do not go and follow such prophets! The day of My Advent will be like a flash of lightning, flashing across the cloudy sky from east to west, illuminating everything under the sky.

However, prior to this, the Son of Man will suffer greatly. He will be completely rejected by this generation, namely the Jews and the Pharisees, and in later times, by those who will be called the new 'Jews and Pharisees.' And as it was at the time of Noah, it will be at the time when the Son of Man will come again. They enjoyed their food and drink, they married and gave in marriage until the day Noah entered the ark and the floods came and drowned all. This is also how it happened at the time of Lot: They ate and drank, planted and cultivated their fields. But on the day Lot left Sodom, it already rained fire and brimstone from the sky, killing all of them.

Behold, thus it will happen also in the times when the Son of Man will be revealed again. Whosoever on that day is on the roof thinking of his possessions in the house, let him not come down from the roof to fetch them. This is to be understood in this manner: Whosoever has a true understanding, let him remain in this understanding and not retreat below it, fearing he might lose worldly advantages through it! For those things will be destroyed. And another metaphor: Whosoever is in the field (of the freedom of cognition), let him not turn back to what is behind him (as old, false doctrines and their dogmas), but let him remember Lot's wife and strive to progress towards truth.

I tell you also this: At that time, two will be at the mill, doing the same work. One shall be accepted, i.e. the righteous worker, and the unrighteous and selfish one will be left. For whosoever will seek to preserve his soul for the sake of the world, shall lose it; but he who will lose it because of the world, shall keep it alive and help it towards true, Eternal Life.

And I also tell you: In one and the same night of the soul, two will be lying in one and the same bed; there too, one will be accepted, the other one left. This means: Outwardly, two will profess to be in the same sphere of faith. One will be active in the living faith and will, therefore, be accepted into God's Kingdom of Life and Light; the other, however, will be adhering only to external cult which has no inner life-value for soul and spirit. Since his faith is dead and without the works of love for his fellowman, he will not be accepted into the living and illuminated Kingdom of God. Further, there will be two working in the field; one of them, who will be working unselfishly in living faith for love of God and love of his neighbour, will be accepted into the true Kingdom of God. And he who will be working in the same field but only for his own self-interest and without inner faith, like the Pharisees, will be left behind and not accepted into God's Kingdom of Life and Light. Behold, this is the way it will be when the Son of Man comes again! If, as a result of this succession, My Spirit will have penetrated you more deeply, then you will have a more illuminated understanding of everything I ever told you. For now, however, I cannot make these proclamations any clearer to you.

If, however, you are so entirely determined to know

about the "when" and "where", then take notice: Where there is a cadaver, the free eagles soon flock together! Now, look at the indolent and faithless pharisaism and you see the cadaver. I, however, and all who believe in Me, Jews and Heathens, are the eagles that will soon consume the cadaver completely. Thus, the soul's night of sin is a cadaver around which the light of life is beginning to spread, destroying the cadaver as the morning annihilates the night with all its mists and illusions. This is now happening before our eyes with the indolent Judaism lacking truth and faith, which has turned into a mighty cadaver, but will in about fifty earth-years come to an end. Thusly, it will also be in later times with the church and its teaching I am now establishing. This too will become an even worse cadaver than Judaism is now. Therefore, the free eagles of light and life will be attacking it from all sides and consuming it as a world-polluting cadaver, with the fire of true love and the might of its light of truth. And it can happen before a full two-thousand years will have passed, counting from the time of My Life on earth, as I have hinted to you already on other occasions.

If, however, in this time, while I am still in the flesh on planet earth, walking among you and teaching, some have already begun to travel in My Name to also spread My Teachings for their own material benefit and have added their own impure seeds, out of which soon will grow plenty of evil weeds amongst the meagre wheat. Will it then be surprising that in later times more false and uncalled-for teachers and prophets will rise in My Name, shouting at the people with mighty words and with the sword in their hands: 'Look! Here is Christ!' or 'there He is!'? If you, and later your descendants, will hear that, do not believe such criers! For by their works they will easily be recognized like the trees by their fruit. A good tree brings forth good fruit, but grapes do not grow on thorned hedges, and on thistles, no figs grow.

However, I have already told you wherein the Kingdom of God consists and how and where it unfolds within man himself. Therefore, you will surely comprehend that those who will be shouting: Look here, look there! cannot be believed. Just as the spirit is within man and all life, and thinking, feeling, knowledge and volition originate from it, thus also God's Kingdom, the true life-realm of the spirit is only within man and not anywhere outside of him. Once a person understands this according to its full living truth, no false prophet will be able to influence him in all eternity. But whosoever, in the understanding of his heart is like a weather-vane or a reed will, of course, hardly be able to find the peaceful haven of life filled with the light of truth! Therefore, you shall be true rocks of life which cannot be moved by storms or great waves!

The Kingdom of God, in Me, has come to you and is now in your midst, but this is not sufficient for gaining and preserving the soul's everlasting life because, although the Kingdom of God, in Me, has come to you it has not yet penetrated your innermost. That can and will only happen when you, without any consideration of the world, will have totally received My Teachings into your will and thus also become fully active in it. Once that is the case, you will no longer say: Christ and with Him the Kingdom of God has come to us and dwells among us. Instead, you will say: I do not live now, but instead Christ lives in me! If this will be the case with you, then you will also fully and vividly comprehend that the Kingdom of God does not come with external pomp to and in man, but only unfolds within man and draws the soul into its Eternal Life."

"Regarding My Words about mankind's state of belief in the distant future when the Son of Man will come to this earth once more, I tell you that, on the whole, He will find even less living faith than now. For in those times people will, through persistent research and calculations under the wide-spread branches of the tree of knowledge, make considerable progress in many of the sciences and the arts. They will accomplish miraculous things with the at-present still unknown natural forces of the earth and will say: Look! That is God, there is no other! Thus, these people will have practically no faith at all and when I return to this earth, I shall no longer find any faith among these people.

Another considerable part of humanity will find themselves in a much denser and darker superstition than all the heathens of the world at this time. These will, for a long time, have their teachers, representatives and protectors in the great and mighty of the earth. But the children of the world, well-equipped with all the sciences and arts, will suppress that dark superstition with great force, thereby considerably embarrassing the great and mighty of the earth. For thanks to science and all the arts, the people who for a long time had been kept in enforced darkness will begin to realize that they have been held in servitude only to serve the worldly honour and opulence of the great and mighty who had no faith themselves. And when I shall then come, I will not find any faith among the people of such a time either! However, once the blind have begun to see the light on account of science, a great number will become followers of those who are mainly responsible for liberating them from the hard servitude of the great and mighty. And if I would then come and say: 'Harken, you nations of the earth! I have now come to you once more and will show you again the right way to the Eternal Life of your souls!' What would those who are bare of faith then say? They would reply to Me like this: 'Friend, whosoever you may be, no more of that old, worn-out and, fortunately evaporated foolishness for the sake of which, since the time of its inception, streams of innocent blood has often been shed. We are now clinging to science and all kinds of arts and through this are living in peace and tranquillity, confident in an only temporal existence. We much prefer a temporal, but peaceful and quite life to a heaven with all its blessings that must be gained through endless suffering and which is still doubtful!'

You say: 'Lord, do not let any false prophets ever arise in Your Name! But if You Yourself want it to be this way, it must be agreeable to You if You do not find any faith among people at the time of Your Future Advent on earth!' To this I say: 'Indeed, it is quite correct that short-sighted human reason judges in accordance to its own insight, and nothing much could be said against it as far as this side of the world is concerned. But God, as the Creator and eternal Preserver of all things and beings, thinks differently and has entirely different ideas and plans with everything He has created out of Himself! And so He also knows best why He allows this or that to happen among the people of this earth. Only in the end will all superstition be swept from the face of the earth with the weapons of the sciences and arts whilst no man will be mislead in the slightest in his free will. The result will eventually be a complete lack of faith among men, but this condition will only exist for a very short duration. In that time, I will bless the ancient tree of knowledge, and the tree of life within man will once more regain its original strength. Then there will be but one shepherd and one fold! In those future times I shall hardly find a faith like the present one, but a different faith! You cannot now imagine what this faith will consist of! Notwithstanding, things will happen as I have now predicted!'

The Teachings I am now giving you are the Word of God and will remain forever. Therefore, those people will also be given the same teachings you have received from Me. However, in those times it will be given to them not veiled but completely revealed according to its heavenly and spiritual meaning. Therein will the new Jerusalem consist which will descend from the heavens to this earth. Only in its light will people realize to what extent their predecessors were deceived by the false prophets, just as the Jews have now been deceived by the Pharisees! Then they will no longer blame Me and My Teachings for all the misery on earth, but only the highly selfish and tyrannical false teachers and prophets and will have recognized exactly what kind of people they were. When, however, the lightest of light of the new Jerusalem shines upon the whole earth, then the liars and deceivers will be completely unmasked and rewarded for their actions. The higher any of them will imagine themselves to be, the lower they will fall."

"I have still many things to say and reveal to you, but you could not bear them yet. But when the spirit of truth, out of Me, will come over you, it will guide you into all truth and wisdom, and then you will be finding yourselves fully within the light of the new Jerusalem. But whether you will then be capable of passing on the light to your disciples is a question that is hard for you to answer. You could now not even imagine the great and comprehensive sciences and crafts future mankind will have developed and how much that will help to thin out all superstition among mankind. But where in all the world can one now speak of a pure science based on the principles of well-calculated truth? And what of crafts derived from such a science? Wherever, among mankind, such a science and art derived therefrom exists, more than three-quarters of these human beings will be insteeped in blind superstition.

However, no higher heavenly truth can be based on such a rotten fruit from the unblessed tree of knowledge. If you would stand on this, a fruit would come into being that could be thrown to the dragons for food, but not serve man as nourishment. See and take note of this: From such fruits also the false prophets will go forth with all their false doctrines and deceptive miracles and spoil more than three-quarters of the earth! For efforts will be made to combine My Purest Teachings of Truth with the sciences that are intermingled with superstition (wrong conclusions) and combining their opinions with rather futile arts, thereby thinking to make it more acceptable to mankind. Thus My Teachings will, naturally, become evermore contaminated. And the sciences and arts, full of superstition, will thereby sink deeper still into the old darkness than they ever have since the beginning of mankind. In the end, for only a span of time, they will become the property of the false prophets so as to make it all the easier for them to win for themselves the people who had been kept in ignorance.

But it will not remain this way. For at the right time, I shall awaken mankind to the pure sciences and arts, and it will be proclaimed from the rooftops how the servants of Balaam have worked their miracles! The pure sciences and the pure arts will thereby become invincible forerunners and pioneers on My behalf against the old superstition. Once the Augean stable will have been cleansed through them, My Return to this earth will be easy and most effective. For My Purest Teachings of Life will easily combine with the pure science of man everywhere, thus giving mankind a complete light of life, because one purity can never contaminate another.

So as to, in time, achieve with mankind a complete cleansing of the sciences and the skills derived therefrom, My

Teachings must first be preached to them and the many idols, together with their priests and temples must be destroyed! Once that has happened and My Gospel has been preached to mankind, even if through many false prophets, only then will they be also capable of gradually cleansing the sciences and arts. These will then be like a flash of lightning brightly illuminating everything on earth from ascent to descent. Ascent denotes the spiritual and descent denotes nature!

A person can never really grasp the deeper transcendental truths to their fullest depth unless he knows the ground upon which he himself stands and walks as a natural man. Therefore, I Myself have already explained many things to you in the field of special phenomena in this world of nature. I have shown you the moon, the sun, all the planets and the entire, endlessly vast starry sky. Thusly, I have told you that a person can only love God totally when he has more and more, in ever-purer concepts, recognized Him in His countless Works. But the main thing is and remains the untiring endeavour for the full rebirth of the spirit within the soul. Only thereby is man exalted to all truth and wisdom. Then he possesses a perfect and coherent light from the earthly into the purely spiritual heavenly, and with the light - also everlasting life. That is then infinitely more than all the sciences about the things of nature! What good would it do a human being if he were able to truly, and in detail, recognize and judge all things and phenomena in nature from the greatest to the smallest, but was still as remote from the rebirth of the spirit within the soul as is this earth from heaven! Would all the sciences be able to gain for him everlasting life?

The ancient science of inner correspondences is open only to those people who have never wavered or weakened in their belief and trust in the One true God, have always loved Him above all as the Father, and have loved their neighbours as themselves. And that, because the aforementioned science constitutes the inner script and language of the soul and its indwelling spirit. Whosoever has lost this language cannot possibly understand its script and, in his dead-worldly light, this language appears to him as foolishness. For the living conditions of the spirit and the soul differ from those of the physical body. This also applies to spiritual hearing, seeing, feeling, thinking, speaking and the script are of a different constitution than those among mankind in the natural world. Therefore, whatever a spirit-entity does and says can be made comprehensible to natural man only by way of the science of correspondences. Mankind lost this science through their own fault. Through this, they have cut themselves off from any communication with the spirits of all the regions and all the heavens and, as a result, can no longer comprehend or grasp the spiritual in the script. They read the written words according to the blind learned sounds of the dead letters, and cannot even comprehend or perceive what is contained therein, that the letters are dead, and that nobody can bring them to life; but, it is only the inner hidden sense of the letter, just as life itself brings everything to life.

If you do comprehend this, strive above all for the rebirth in the spirit so that the Kingdom of God can become alive and fully active within you. Then you will once more reach the science of correspondences between matter and spirit. Without it you cannot ever understand Moses or any of the prophets in the depth of living truth, but will sink into unbelief, doubt and sin instead of escaping the numerous dangers threatening to engulf you.

I have shown you now clearly enough how and in what way I shall return to humanity on this earth.

On the occasion of My Second Coming, I shall not again be born as a child of a woman anywhere, for My Body remains transfigured as do I as a spirit in eternity, and so I shall not ever again need another body like the one I have now on earth. First I shall come invisibly in the "clouds of heaven", which means to say: I shall first approach humanity through true seers, wise men and newly-awakened prophets. And in those days also maidens will prophesy and young men will have clairvoyant dreams announcing My Advent. Many will listen to them and mend their ways, but the world will call them mad dreamers and not believe them, as was also the case with the prophets.

Thusly I will, from time to time, awaken human beings to whom I will dictate, through their heart into their pen, all that which is now, during My Presence here, occurring and being spoken. Human beings in those days, almost all of whom will be able to read and write, will be able to read and also understand the new books. This way of spreading My Teachings from the heavens given anew and pure, will then make it possible to reach people all over the earth much more quickly and effectively than is now possible through messengers in My Name by word of mouth.

When in this manner, My Teachings will have been brought among people of good will and active faith and at least one-third of humanity will have knowledge of it. Then I will also, here and there, come personally and become bodily visible to those who love Me most, and who have the greatest yearning for My Return, and will have a fully alive faith. And I Myself shall form of them congregations which no power on earth will be able to resist. For I shall be their Commander-In-Chief, their forever-invincible Hero, and shall judge all the dead and blind worldlings. Thusly I will cleanse the earth of its ancient filth.

At the time of the new seers and prophets, however, there will be great tribulations and sorrow among the people as has never before been the case on this earth. But for the sake of My Chosen Ones this will be only of short duration, so that they do not come to grief in their progress toward salvation. However, in this land where I am now being persecuted like a criminal by the Jews of the temple, and pursued from one place to another, and which at that time will be trampled underfoot by the darkest heathens, I shall not at first appear personally. But in the lands of another continent, which at present is inhabited by heathens, I shall establish a new Kingdom: A Kingdom of Peace, Harmony, Love and Lasting-Living Faith. There will no longer be any fear of the death of the body among men who walk in My Light, and who will be in constant contact with the angels of heaven.

The earth is Mine everywhere, and I know where My Return will be most effective for all the earth. But in those days when people will be able to communicate with each other from one end of the earth to the other with lightning speed and, by making use of the spirits bound in the fire and water, will be able to travel across the longest stretches of the earth faster than the fiercest storm; and when also ships, by means of the same forces, will cross the oceans in the shortest time, it will be possible to easily spread the news of My Personal Return within a very short time over the entire earth, and also to Asia.

But there remains the question: Will the news be believed by the blind and deaf heathens of this continent? I should say: Hardly, until it will have been cleansed through a Great Universal Judgment!

There is a vast land in the far west, which is on all sides surrounded by oceans and does not anywhere connect with the old world above water. From this land (America), people will first be hearing great things, and these things will also appear in the west of Europe. The result will be bright, radiating and reflecting rays: The lights of heaven will meet, recognize and support each other. Out of these lights, the Sun of Life will be forming, which is the new, perfect Jerusalem, and in this Sun I shall return to earth. This visible heaven and this earth will eventually pass away, but My Words which I have spoken to you will not pass!"

A PORTRAYAL OF MANKIND'S DEVELOPMENT

*Jesus speaks to His disciples
about the happenings prior to His Advent,
while they all watch a sunrise.*

"With My Birth, the judgment of the heathens everywhere has already begun. Now this will be continuing on a larger scale for almost 2000 years until the full light will have spread among the people on this earth! In the east, as you can now see, all kinds of clouds are amassing on the horizon - as if they wanted to obstruct the rising of the sun. Thusly, in days to come, also a great mass of various obstructing clouds will begin to tower up against the coming great rise of the spiritual and eternal Sun of Truth and cause much harm among mankind. However, it will be unable to finally prevent the great rise of the Sun of Truth. Earlier, you still saw many beautiful stars shining in the firmament, and in the west, stars which had been shining in the deep night. Behold, they preceded the still-visible heralds of the morning and were working in the night. And this is now your task!

When, however, on the spiritual horizon of the morning, the even-lighter harbingers of the morning ascend, that will be a sign that soon will follow The Great Universal Sun of Truth and Life. Its brilliant light will be an inexorable judgment of all falsehood and deceit, out of which the whore of Babel was formed who, with all her disciples and admirers, as well as her worldly pomp, will be thrown into the abyss of contempt, just wrath and oblivion. Then the enlightened human beings will no longer reflect upon the deceit and the long-lasting judgment.

Now you can already notice how the earlier, threatening black clouds begin to develop a golden lining. In those days, you will notice how people who not too long ago were true enemies of the light of truth, are now being enlightened more and more from all sides by the light-rays of truth and as a result become self-luminous and enemies of the old falsehood. And such an illumination from the approaching Sun of Truth from the heavens towards the full rising will be My sign of the

Son of Man for all followers of truth on the earth, and the beginning of the end of the great judgment over the whore of the new Babel. (Matthew 24:30)

Then the lovers of truth will be rejoicing and praising Me for having sent them, already in advance, the sign of My Ascension in the heavens of the inner day of the spirit. The enemies of truth, however, will be beginning to weep and gnash their teeth. They will be trying, wherever possible, to hide in dark corners with their ever-decreasing number of faithful, but in vain. For once the full Sun of Truth will have risen, its light will be illumining even the remotest nooks, corners and caves, and the enemies of the light will no longer find a refuge anywhere on earth.

I, Myself, will be in that Sun as the Eternal Truth. Through its light, I will be the Ruler of Mankind, and also the Guide of their lives and their temporal and eternal destinies. Thus I have now shown you truthfully and comprehensibly the great judgment of the new and old heathendom. This was for you; but later on I shall give you yet another picture for the people which you may pass on, but not without the true interpretation. But now let us continue to watch the morning scene. Pay good attention to all the phenomena that will still be emerging prior to the full sunrise! For I wish that you, too, should see with your eyes how things will turn out during the latter days of the new heathendom."

(First a dense and completely black fog could be seen rising above the horizon. When this fog had reached approximately seven times the height of the distant mountain range on the horizon, it appeared to glow, for countless flashes of lightning were traversing it. And on the black upper top edge of the fog mass, which was glowing because of the many flashes of lightning, there appeared a big city.)

And I said: "Look at the picture of the new Babel! That is the decline of the old and simultaneously the beginning of the new heathendom. In about five to six hundred years from now it will really look like that. But continue to watch the formation!" Again, all of them focused their attention on the formation whose scenes kept developing in quick succession. Great movements of nations could be seen, and bitter battles and wars. In the middle of the city, something rose high like a mountain and upon it was a high and large throne as of glowing gold. Seated on the throne was a ruler with a triple crown on his head and a staff with a triple cross adorning its top. Countless arrows were shooting from his mouth and as many lightnings of anger and utmost pride were flashing from his eyes and chest. And kings were approaching him, many of whom were bowing deeply before him. Upon those he looked kindly, confirming their might, but the ones who did not bow to him were badly pursued and harmed by his arrows and lightnings.

Said I: "This does not show a particular ruler over many lands and nations, but only the visible personification of the Antichrist! The triple cross, however, denotes My Teachings which will be imposed upon the kings and their nations in a threefold adulteration: False in the word, false in the truth, and false in the living practice.

Those kings who do not bow to him and whom he curses are those who are still more or less abiding by the old teaching. His arrows and flashes of lightning do reach them, yet not enough to inflict extensive harm. Now, continue to observe the eidetic events, and through this I can show you only the most important moments!"

Once more they all observed the scene with heightened attentiveness. "And behold, many of the kings, who earlier had still bowed deeply to the one on the throne, were now gathering their armies and marching against him. Look, there is a fierce battle and his high throne is already sinking considerably deeper into the city. You now see only a few kings who are still bowing to him for appearance's sake, but many arrows and flashes of lightning are being returned to him by those who deserted him. And now not much more can be seen of him. All this will be already occurring in 1000-1500-1600 and 1700 years.

Look, now he is attempting to rise again, surrounded by black hordes, and some kings are extending their hands to help him. But those who are doing so will soon be totally unconscious, and their nations are tearing the crowns from their heads and giving them to the powerful kings! And look! - now the throne is sinking, and the strong kings are hurrying towards it, and divide it into several parts. Thus, all his might, loftiness and grandeur is coming to an end. Although he is still shooting arrows and there are still weak flashes of lightning all around him, they no longer harm anybody, for most of them are returning, wounding him and his weak and sinister hordes."

"What do the 'light clouds' denote? They are communities of human beings who are illumined by Divine Truth. Now all of them are moving closer together, thus forming one large community, and this is the new earth above which a new heaven, full of light and clearness, is unfolding!

However, you must not be of the opinion that this natural earth will be passing away and be changed into a new one. Only those human beings who, through the full acceptance in their hearts of Divine Truth, will be considered true brothers and sisters among themselves by creating in My Name a new spiritual earth.

On this new earth, I Myself will be present and will govern among My Own, and they will associate with Me and never lose sight of Me.

Look how increasingly dense streams of light are floating from this new earth down towards the old earth, igniting it so that it appears to be ablaze! You see many dead coming forth from their graves towards the light - how they are soon clothed with the Garment of Truth and then ascend to the realm of the new earth. At the same time you also notice how a considerable number of sinister souls endeavour to don the garment of light over their dark one in order to thereby create once more an anti-christian heathendom out of self-interest and a lust for power. But I Myself will let My Wrath come over them, i.e. the fire of My Truth. And My angels are descending upon them as if with flaming swords, forcing any further sinister efforts into the abyss, for complete annihilation. This is then the final and greatest judgment about one-thousand years later. This time will be called My Thousand-Year-Reign on earth, which will be interrupted once by warfare for a very short time, due to this last and final judgment. But soon a complete victory will be gained for all future times.

From then on, out of the heavens and the earth, there will be one shepherd and one fold. As at all times, I shall be the Shepherd and the fold will consist of humanity on earth, fully united with the blessed in My Heavens. The latter will again visibly associate with men on earth as it used to be in the early times of mankind. However, prior to this, also the natural earth will suffer from mighty changes. Vast lands and empires which are, at present, still covered by the great and deep oceans will rise, offering the most fertile soil. Many now still high mountains will be levelled, filling deep chasms and valleys with their crumbled peaks and will form fertile land.

Since in those days mankind will no longer be coveting earthly, perishable treasures, just as many people as at present will be living on the earth, well-provided for and happy. Also, at the same time, all the bad diseases which torment the flesh so mightily will vanish from the earth. Mankind will reach a happy and great age and will be able to do a lot of good. No one will fear the death of the physical body because he will have before him a clear conception of the Eternal Life of the soul.

In those times, the main emphasis in regards to helping your fellowman will be placed on properly rearing children, and on the strong and healthy supporting those who are physically old and weak with all their love and strength. Marriage on this blissful earth will be ordained, as it is in heaven in accordance to My Order. And a great number of children will be procreated but not by way of sheer lewdness, but by way of the true earnestness of love, and that until the end of the earth.

Now you have a true picture of the last judgment of all the heathens on the whole of planet earth which you should understand very easily and well."

"Here the disciples asked Me: 'Lord and Master! Will we too be able to see and experience all that from the realm of the spirits? And how long will this blissful earth still continue to exist until the full end of its time?'

Said I: 'As for your question, it goes without saying that you will, from the heavens, not only clearly see, hear and feel all of that, but you will be the chief leaders there and at all times; not just on the new earth, but for the entire, great Man of Creation (the Macrocosm) as well as for the countless societies of all the heavens which are not ever limited anywhere.'

That is why I say to you: 'No human being has ever seen or heard, nor has one human being since ever perceived what God has prepared for those who truly love Him! I could still tell you and show you many things, but you could not bear it yet. However, when the Spirit of all Truth and Life will come over you, and you will have been reborn in the spirit, it will guide you into all depths of My Light and exalt you. Only then will you understand the Great Words I have now spoken to you and through you to all of mankind!

Concerning your second question; it is truly still unwise. For our account does not contain a numeral by which the vast number of earth-years could be determined which will still have to elapse until the end of time. And even if it were possible, it would be all the same to those who are living on in the spirit.

If you carefully take into consideration My Commandments of true and pure neighbourly love, you will easily comprehend that every genuine and true human being is being hurt most by the pride of his fellowman. Therefore, everyone should be full of gentleness and humility, and through this you will bestow to each other the greatest of honour and live together in peace and tranquillity.

Ambition and pride, however, produce sullenness, annoyance, contempt, resentment, rage, and finally, vengeance and war with all its evil consequences. The arrogant and ambitious are also full of selfishness and avarice. And since they want to gain everything just to enhance their worldly importance, the sad consequence will be that thousands around them will have to live in the greatest of poverty and need, as was the case at the time of Noah, and will be even more so in the latter days of the new heathendom.

This evil and hellish state among mankind will be the judgment they will be preparing for themselves! The vast number of oppressed and poor will finally rise against their arrogant oppressors and do away with them. That will be a second Deluge through the fire of wrath of the in-the-end too-severely oppressed poor.

Also, a natural fire will at that time devastate many places. For in those days, out of exaggerated worldly greed mankind, like evil worms, will be penetrating into the depths of the earth, there to seek and also find, all kinds of treasures. However, once they will have reached the mighty deposits of the earth's primeval buried forests - which they will be using for heating, the melting of metals and many other things - then the final judgment they have prepared for themselves will be at their door. Those who will be living in the large cities of the earth's mighty will have to suffer most. That is why all of you should remain at all times in gentleness and humility, and thereby in the true love of your neighbour, then there will not be any judgment among you. For where in those days people will be living within My Order, no final judgment will come to pass."

BIBLICAL INTERPRETATIONS

1.

*"I will not leave you comfortless;
I will come to you."*
(John 14:18)

"Wherein will an influence by the Holy Spirit be recognizable in the time referred to? Perhaps in the worldly-wise state and warfare laws or even in the manifold canonical disciplinary laws? Not at all! Because I am not the reason for all of this, but worldly benefits for sovereigns. All of them strive for power; emperor, king, prince and, more or less, all those below them. There has to be an emperor, a king, a prince; not for the sake of domination, but that the nations, through their guidance, are being led to Me. However, this way they are only diverted from Me and are being directed to the world; they are not made strong, but only weak, so that in their weakness they are all the easier to govern. Is this the effectiveness of the Holy Spirit, if the monarch regards his underlings as a kind of serf who can, at any time, be destroyed by his word, should it suit him? The monarch is meant to be a guide and comforter to his people and to give them laws that are based on Mine! Then he would be a proper monarch and the Holy Spirit would be working with him as was once the case with worthy monarchs. But the Holy Spirit is never at work in the invention of all kinds of machines, superseding the work of human hands, in the excessive advancement of industry, in activating a great military power! All that was also customary at the time of Noah prior to the Deluge, under the influence of the spirit of the world representing the devil in his totality. The same was the case in Sodom and Gomorrah, and in Babel.

Who would want to maintain that this was the work of the Holy Spirit? Therefore, this is why such actions which were contrary to the Holy Spirit, were always followed by a mighty judgment. Such a judgment I am now holding in readiness in order to demonstrate that My Holy Spirit is nowhere present in the actions of the world today and the world stands, as a result, totally orphaned.

For awhile I still allow it to continue until it will have reached the highest peak before falling. Then there will be a flash of lightning from dawn to dusk, in the light of which it will become evident how many there are in the world! If this is the case, where will then be those I do not wish to leave comfortless? I tell you: 'There are some here and some there, but they have now become almost rarer than crown jewels. They lead a simple life as much as possible secluded from the world. Their joy and the subject of their discussion am I! For out of the abundance of the heart the mouth speaketh. These are indeed not orphans, for I am among them and teach them personally. They hear My Voice at all times, which they recognize as being the Voice of the Rightful Shepherd, and not as that of a hireling which they would not follow, as it would be the voice of a false prophet. They are also the ones for whom My Word is given. I am, therefore, not in need of worldly scholars or law-givers, but only of humble hearts that love Me. Where I find such, I will add everything else and that, to be sure, in a better way than the world could invent. Then everything will be under the influence of the Holy Spirit, and there will no longer be any orphans in the world. Verily, there are at present only very few whose ear is receptive to My Voice!'"

2.

*"And then shall appear
the sign of the Son of Man in heaven."
(Matthew 24:30)*

"Do you not know the difference which exists between the signs and the Son of Man? And do you not know what is to be understood as "heaven"? Truly, you could not imagine anything more foolish than a crucifix becoming visible in the starry sky. Ask yourselves, what good would it do to the world, even if not just one, but a multitude of crosses were to become visible in the sky? Would that make people better in their hearts? Oh no, truly not! Would not the scholars soon declare all these crucifixes to be phantoms of deceit, and prove that all the crosses in the sky have but an aerostatic origin! Behold such an effect, and similar ones, an appearance like that would bring forth in the learned world. Indeed, mathematicians may also endeavour to explain such appearances by way of optics. And what would the man in the street say to it? He would, I assure you, become silent with extreme fear. Because of the false doctrines instilled in him, he would be certain that the Last Judgment Day was standing before his door. So, this would be the effect of such an appearance.

If events would occur in that manner, you could gather, if you would direct your attention toward those periods in time where certain dubious prophets had already several times predicted the end of the world. How on those occasions some people were in despair, others laughed and others again submitted to gluttony and all kinds of debauchery! But if already idle prophecies brought forth such evil appearances, what would happen if a giant cross appeared under the stars?

However, the meaning of "heaven" is the entire religious faith out of the Word which is the church in its genuineness. The sign of the Son of Man is out of this church newly-awakened love with all its heavenly attributes such as: Mercy, Patience, Gentleness, Humility, Submission, Obedience, and Tolerance of all the burdens of the cross. Behold, this living sign of the Son of Man will be appearing in the heaven of the inner Eternal Life, and it will not destroy, but enliven considerably. On this occasion the worldly-minded people on earth will, indeed, be weeping, moaning and lamenting since all of their hellish deceit will no longer take its normal course. Those of My sign will no longer have anything to do with the world-merchants, brokers, and money-changers, for they will be directing their eyes only to where they will see the Son of Man coming in the clouds of heaven with great power and glory; namely, in the living Word in the hearts of mankind, which is My Eternal Love in its fullest essence and, therefore, of great power and glory. The "clouds of heaven" are the infinite wisdom itself within this living Word.

Behold, this is briefly the understanding of this scripture

text. In the beyond, however, these clouds will be receiving you into My Kingdom and will be your everlasting dwelling. That is, only there, in supreme bliss, will you fully see and recognize the great power and glory of the Son of Man."

3.

"Lo, I am with you always."
(Matthew 28:20)

"You shall not have only one, but several signs showing you at all times that I am always in spirit with you, among you, and present within you! These never-failing signs will be forever as follows:

Firstly, that you love Me more than anything in the world. For if someone loves something in the world more than Me, he is not worthy of Me. But he who truly loves Me above everything is, through such true love, within Me and I am within him.

A second sign of My Presence with you shall be that, out of love for Me, you love also your fellowman, young and old, as yourself. Whosoever does not love his fellowman whom he sees, how can he love God in Me, whom he does not see? Although you now see Me and hear Me, from now on you will no longer be seeing Me in this world. And when you will no longer see Me, will your love remain the same as it is now when you are seeing Me? This love will be remaining with you, but make certain that it remains also with your descendants! If one will truly love Me above all in his heart and through this, live and act in accordance with My Revealing Will, I will come to him in the spirit as if personally and reveal My Presence to him.

A third sign of My Presence within and among you shall also be that you are at all times given everything for which you in all earnest ask the Father within Me in My Name! However, it goes without saying that you shall not ask for idle things of this world. For if you did so, you would only reveal that you love such things more than Me. This would truly then not be a sign of My Presence among you.

A fourth sign of My mighty Presence shall also be this: if, out of true love for your fellowman you will, in My Name, lay your hands upon physically sick human beings, they will improve, provided it serves towards the salvation of their soul. But you shall always say in your heart: 'Lord, not mine, but Your Will be done!' For you cannot know whether and when the healing of the body will serve the soul to gain salvation. No one will live forever on this earth in the physical body, and the laying-on-of-hands will not always relieve every human being of his body's ailments. But you will not commit a sin if you render your appropriate love to every ailing person, for I will provide the ability, as long as it serves the soul's salvation, which I alone can know.

If you have heard that a far-away friend is ill, do pray for him and in your mind lay your hands upon him, and he could improve. The prayer in your heart shall then consist of the following few words: 'may Jesus, the Lord, help you! May He strengthen you, may He heal you through His grace, love and mercy!' If you speak these words full of faith and trust in Me over a sick person, however distant he may be from you, and in your mind you hold your hands over him, he will get better within the hour if that should serve towards his soul's salvation.

A fifth sign of My Presence will be if you always do My Will, you will achieve the rebirth of the spirit within you. When you then are filled with My Spirit and are thereby enlightened with all wisdom, it will be a true baptism of life for you. Let everyone strive above all for this fifth sign! If it proves true within him, he will have gained Eternal Life already in this world. He will be able to do and create what I am doing and creating because he will be at one with Me. Now I have shown you the signs of My Presence. Act accordingly, and you will soon become truly aware of My Spirit within you and among you.

I shall remain with My Own in spirit, in the Word and in truth! And those who love Me very much will sometimes also get to see Me personally for a moment. With those who live according to My Word and earnestly search for the inner truth, I will speak through the understanding of their hearts and put

My Words into their minds. Young men and maidens well brought up in My Name shall have visions in which My Being, the heavens and Eternal Life, as well as the lot of the faithless and evil, will be explained to them. And thus I will remain with My Own to the end of this earth!"

THE "ANTICHRIST"

(Received through Gottfried Mayerhofer 1871)
(Text: The Revelation of John, Chapter 11)

"First of all, I make it comprehensible to you that in My Teachings and Words lie considerably more salvation and blessings, if lived accordingly, than if you could interpret all the vials of wrath in the prophecies of John.

This much I can tell you: The earth, with its entire humanity, is engaged in the process of separation, and that everything which is going to happen soon is, indeed, written in those prophecies, but it will not be fulfilled in the sense in which you would interpret it. To "shorten the days" means - in view of the spreading of My Word - to speed up the cleansing of the earth of its corruptible elements, which has already been taking place for some time.

You also keep reading of the "Antichrist"; most people imagine this to be a personality. If they looked upon the world with an attentive eye, they would find many "anti-christians", because there are only very few actual successors of Christ or My Teachings, and even these are still far from being what they really should be.

The actual "Antichrist" is the generally prevailing obsession for entirely different things than are preached by My Teachings. It is the prevailing inclination of so many people where only the head is active and the heart is being condemned to silence. Here you must accept the "head" or the calculating intellect (as the spiritual principle) as the "Antichrist" who has already for a long time been actively working his wiles on earth, endeavouring to explain to mankind, by seductive arguments, that only what the intellect can grasp and elucidate is true.

Whereas, what the heart feels or suspects is nothing but the fleeting haze of an excited imagination! That is why the doctrine of the materialists is the last stage of rationalistic wisdom, and therefore, the addiction to pleasure and the means by which to satisfy it, and the contempt for all which is noble, good and sublime. Thusly, "knowledge and no faith"! And still man forgets what I once said: 'Your knowledge is but fragmented!'

All these pictures in the Apocalypse of John are spiritual figures. They are prevailing epidemic mental disorders which drive and dominate people. In order to be able to decode these revelations, a person must think on a much higher level than he is capable of at this stage. He must see and understand, from My standpoint, the spiritual inner world of the souls enveloped in a physical body on earth. He must recognize how the spiritual trend changes, how I then make use of it for My Own purposes and how, instead of what mankind would like to achieve, only My Great Goal can be strived for! If he is capable of rising to this point of view, then he will also understand what it means: "They killed the prophets and left their dead bodies lying in the street for three and one-half days." This signifies: When mankind heard the teachings of My Chosen Ones, they refused to accept them, mocked My scribes and servants, or regarded them as non-existent, as dead. They rejected My Teachings or 'left them lying on the open street', not believing in them, but also not completely discarding them either. Until after a short time (figuratively three and one-half days) truth triumphed again, the one believed dead became alive once more and returned to whence he had come, i.e. he ascended to Me. Whosoever comprehends the meaning of these words, that is, what they signify spiritually, will also easily find out the meaning of "the city of Babylon" or "the place of intellectual errors."

Whosoever throws himself into My Arms can calmly watch the coming events. He knows that it is all for the benefit of the straying children. Once he will realize from My Words that the world cannot exist in this way - since I did not create it for this purpose - he will also understand that I have to return, in order to save whatever can still be saved! Wherefore he, too, shall strive only for no other goal, than to prepare himself so as to be worthy of and be counted as one of "My Children", and not be swept away from the earth and annihilated with the rest of the debris!"

THE PRESENT SPIRITUAL DELUGE

(Received through Jakob Lorber 1849)

He Who has created, delivered and sanctified you through His Word and through His Spirit, is telling you:

"A spiritual deluge is now wafting across the earth as the flood of four thousand earth-years ago once did at the time of Noah. That one killed the flesh, but this one kills the soul and the body. The soul kills this flood through the spirit of lust for power which now spurts forth from the interior of the earth and out of the air, as once the undulation of water did. That means the evil spirits come forth out of these elements and flood the soul and corrupt her with the lust for power.

This flood is like a fire, and is the very same fire of which it is written (II Epistle Peter, Chapter 3) that the world at large will thereby be judged for a second time. Abide with Me, if you do not wish to be seized by this awful flood of fire. Do not judge one day this way and one day that way, or say: This one or that one, this or that party, or the high or the lowborn are right. For I tell you: Nobody is right now, except he who does not bend hither or thither, but stays with Me - straight and firm as a rock - leaving everything to Me. What is beyond that, is sin!

All of this had to happen for the sake of the Word of God, which is My Word, spoken by Me for Jerusalem about Jerusalem and, as such, over the whole world. Great events will occur: You will see and hear much evil. One nation will condemn another and one party will erect gallows for the other. Those who shortly before greeted one another as friends will betray each other: the son the father and the father the son! However, judge no one but leave everything to Me, and you will find yourselves in My Ark of Peace, where no evil of this time will touch you.

Who among you has the power to be of real consequence in the world? If he judges the party which is in the end victorious, will they not seize him and demand justification? If, on the other hand, he sides with the others and the first party wins, will this party not also do what the other did to the one who was against it? Up to now I have not predetermined victory to any party except to the one that adheres to Me, therefore, refrain equally from praise and from reproach! Only I know whom you should praise or criticize, and I shall give to each according to his deeds!

Should, however, one power be victorious, just obey the power which has won the victory, for it could not be a power unless it was ordained by Me! If I accepted the judgment of Pilate and did not resist, even though it concerned My Own Body, you need not fear for your safety and grumble at what is going to happen. No sparrow falls from the roof without My Will, and even all the hairs on your head are counted. How should all these events happen without My Volition? If it is My Will because the world has willed it so, and stills wills it, it is likewise My Concern to protect those who adhere to Me and leave everything to Me. Do you not know that My Counsel is inexplicable and My Ways unfathomable?

I need not repeat to you all that is going to happen. For a great deal can happen, or very little, as to whether the people will turn to Me or against Me. The sword has already wreaked havoc, and will continue to drive human beings into a flood of their lust for power. I shall send them yet another angel, namely the Angel of Hunger and, at the same time, the Angel of Pestilence. These lessons will teach people concepts entirely different from those they are now holding.

Your motto should be: "Render unto Caesar what is his, but above all to Me what is Mine!" In this way, you will live in peace with the world and with Me, and will in everything truly be My Children. Amen."

THE POWERS OF HEAVEN WILL BE SHAKEN

My Children! It is written: "And the powers of heaven will be shaken." That is why many human beings believe that the stars will fall down from heaven; but this will not happen, for it has an entirely different meaning.

Souls from so many planets and solar worlds have now been incarnated on earth. Many of these souls have become immersed in the grossest materialism, having completely lost the belief in a supreme, personified deity while, in, fact they came here to search for this very same deity. Their relatives, even all inhabitants of those worlds, are praying incessantly for those who went out to find the "Great Spirit" as the "Good, Tender-Loving Father", and bring back to them news of Him. What, however, will such a soul say when it returns? Many do not return at all after their physical death, because they became too closely attached to materialism. These beings will, through My Mercy, go to a place where they gradually become purified and free.

Now, those who came from above should find the way to Me and also should show it to those who came from below. But many times, it is those who came from above who have brought all this wrongness and misery to this earth. Now the time has come when I shall give a view of the earth to the inhabitants of the larger planets and suns, and I will describe to them the viewpoint of those who have come to earth in search of Me. Due to this, they will certainly be severely irritated; this irritation will extend from Venus to Urka.[3] Thus, it will come to pass that "the powers of the heavens will be shaken", and there will be a mighty call from all directions to the inhabitants of this earth. A spirit will blow them all down, and a storm will rage from east to west, bending all stubborn and strong spirits, and nothing will be able to resist this mighty storm. It is then I shall come to those who are Mine as their holy Father. Amen!

---

[3]Urka (UR = light; KA = energy) is in the constellation of Leo with its principal star Regulus. (Ed.)

THE THOUSAND-YEAR KINGDOM
(THE MILLENNIUM)

(Received through Jakob Lorber in 1864)

"I have seen to it that I, as the only true Christ, shall attain among human beings recognition of the true inner life. And that will be the true rock which the powers of hell will not overcome: I shall be the cornerstone which the many builders have cast hither and thither. Woe betide him who will take offence at that cornerstone, he will be shattered to pieces like a fragile jar. He on whom the cornerstone will fall will be crushed to dust and ashes! And this is how My up-to-now misunderstood Thousand-Year-Reign will come.

Anyone who carefully examines the ancient Arabic ciphers will, by way of analogy, see in their configuration something other than the one-thousand units of the number 'one-thousand'.

The number "one" in the number 1000 represents Me in My human personality and the three zeros following the "one" represent Me in the fullness of My Divine Trinity. Thus, the expression "One-Thousand Years" means that the number 1000 represents Me in the fullness of My Divinity, represented accordingly.

But the word 'year' denotes the time during which I shall remain first in command to the end, guiding and leading the nations of this earth, partly Myself and partly through many of My newly-awakened servants. They (the people of the thus-blessed period) will also have to go through a probation for their freedom of life, just as they now have a hard battle with materialism. But after having survived the battle, they will be clothed in the Garment of Immortality. You are therefore living in The Great Transitional Period.

Happy is he who believingly accepts these things in his heart without being angry at the many devilries perpetrated in this world. They will not last long, for I shall cut them short for the sake of My Chosen Ones who will then praise Me and rejoice. I shall not cast righteous rulers from their thrones but shall fill them with My Spirit, whereupon there will be one flock and one shepherd, so that what I have prophesied to the people during My earthly lifetime will be fulfilled."

THE SEVENFOLD COMING OF THE LORD

(From "The Household of God", Chapter 46)
Early History of Mankind
(Received through Jakob Lorber 1840)

"I shall come seven times; but at the seventh time I shall come in the fire of My Holiness. Woe betide those who will be found unrighteous; they will be no more, except in the eternal fire of My wrath!

Behold, I have once been here in the beginning of the world, to create all things for your sake, and you for Mine. Soon I shall return in great floods of water in order to wash the pestilence off the earth; for the depths of the earth have become an abomination before Me, full of dirty mire and pestilence, which has come forth out of your disobedience. There I shall come for your sake so that the whole world may not perish and one lineage shall remain of which I Myself shall be the last offspring.

And I shall come for the third time to you many times as I have come to you countless times now - sometimes visibly and sometimes invisibly in the Word of the Spirit - to prepare My Way. I shall come a fourth time bodily, in great need, in the great time of times. And I shall come immediately after that for the fifth time in the spirit of love and all sanctification (Pentecost). And I shall come for the sixth time to the inner self of anyone who has a true and serious yearning for Me in his heart, and I shall be a guide to him who, full of love and faith, will let himself be drawn to an Eternal Life by Me. At that time I shall be more remote from the world; but whosoever will be accepted will live, and My Kingdom will be with him forever.

Finally, I shall come once again, as it has been said before; but this last coming will be to all a permanent coming - one way or another! Listen and comprehend well: Abide in love, for this will be your Redeemer. Love Me above all; this will be your life Everlasting. Love also one another so that you will be released from judgment. My grace and first love be with you until the end of all times! Amen."

THE GREAT AND NEW JERUSALEM

[The Lord]: "I am the pillar of light *(refers to a previous light phenomenon which the Lord interprets for His disciples according to its spiritual correspondence)* returned from the heavens to this earth, in the spirit of My Living Word which in the future I shall lay in the hearts of those human beings who will love Me and keep My Commandments. To those I shall come and reveal Myself. And thus they will all be taught anew by God.

The division of the pillar into innumerable parts signifies the unveiling of the inner, spiritual meaning of all My Words and Teachings which I have given to human beings since the beginning of mankind, through the mouth of the patriarchs, the prophets and seers, and now through Myself.

Out of the many partial unveilings of the inner spiritual sense of the Word of God will then be formed a true and great light and life doctrine which will descend from the heavens to human beings. And those who will live according to the New Teachings will walk and live eternally in the New Jerusalem, and there will be blissfulness upon blissfulness, without measure, aim or end. For I Myself shall be with them, and they will behold all the innumerable splendours of My love, wisdom, and omnipotence.

There will be very little light amongst the people of earth counting from the fall of this old city of Jerusalem to the time of God's New City on earth. For only too soon there will rise plenty of false prophets and priests in My Name, and they will work false miracles and blind and beguile the people - indeed, the Antichrist will, with the aid of the rulers of the earth, perpetrate things which could even seduce My Chosen Ones into kneeling before the new Baal, provided I permitted it. But then I shall again send great hardships among the people such as has never before been seen under the sun. Then Baal will be overthrown like the great whore of Babel, and the light of the living word will then come into the hearts of many people and will comfort and redeem those troubled and oppressed, and all will rejoice in the new light and praise My Name.

In those times, many people will communicate with the

pure spirits of My heaven who, as their teachers, will instruct them in all secrets of the Eternal Life in God, as was shown to you in the third coming when you saw people walk in and out through the twelve gates.

However, the twelve gates will now no longer bear witness that the new city be built from the twelve tribes of Israel, but from the twelve main principles of My Teachings, which are contained in the Ten Commandments of Moses and in My Two new Commandments of Love; for these are the gates by which the people will in the future enter God's new, enlightened and true-to-life City.

Only he who will keep these My Commandments will enter this city, and he will be given light and life; but he who will not keep them, will not gain entrance to this new city. Therefore, the twelve kinds of precious stones out of which the wall around the great city was built, again signify the same Twelve Commandments.

These Twelve Commandments are, therefore, not only the entrance gates to the light and life for human beings, but they are also our indestructible protection and shelter which the gates and powers of hell or the material worldliness can never destroy or conquer.

At the same time, did you notice when you observed the apparition, how the stones of the wall gave off a powerful light in all its colors. This is an indication for you that the Twelve Commandments given to you are also contained in all degrees of Divine Wisdom and only through keeping the Twelve Commandments, can human beings reach perfect wisdom. For in the Commandments is contained all wisdom from God, and as all of God's Wisdom is contained therein, so is all divine power and strength, because in these Commandments there is the most wise and Almighty Will and through this is contained the highest freedom.

Whosoever, therefore, has made God's Will his own by keeping the Commandments, has also made the divine power and divine freedom his own, has reached the phase of true rebirth of the spirit and is, as a true child of God, as perfect as the Father in heaven Himself.

I am telling all of you now, through keeping the Commandments in the minutest of detail, you should above all endeavour to reach perfection while here on earth - perfection just like the Father in Heaven. Then you will be able to do what I am doing now, but you will be able to do even greater things. And once you find yourselves at this phase, you will then be citizens of the New Jerusalem beforehand."

INTERPRETATION OF
THE SECOND CHAPTER OF ISAIAH

[The Lord]: "The word that Isaiah, the son of Amoz, saw concerning Judah and Jerusalem. And it shall come to pass in the last days, that the mountain of the Lord's House shall be established in the top of the mountains, and shall be exalted above the hills; and all heathens shall flow unto it."

Behold, I am the mountain of all mountains on which stands the true House of God. But what is the house? It is My Word, which I have spoken for several centuries through all the prophets to you Jews, and which I Myself am now speaking through the mouth of the Son of Man. Therefore, I am the mountain, and My Word is the habitable house on the mountain, and around us are gathered the heathens from all corners of the earth who have come here to inspect the mountain and take lodging in its vast house. But for the Jews, as they are now, these are truly the last days because they flee the mountain and its house, and the high and mighty even threatening to destroy it.

But Isaiah continues as follows: "And many nations shall (i.e. in the future) come and say: Come, let us climb up onto the mountain of the Lord, to the house of the God of Jacob, that He may teach us His Ways, and we may walk in His Paths. For the law will come out of Zion, and out of Jerusalem comes the Word of the Lord!"

There should not be any doubt now that by Zion (Z'e on = He will) is to be also understood the mountain, the Lord, or I, and by Jerusalem - the House of God on the mountain; therefore, My Word and My Teachings for now and forever.

But who are the nations who say: "Come let us climb up onto the mountain of the Lord, that is, to the Son of Man or God Incarnate, and to the house of the God of Jacob, that He may teach us His Ways and we may walk in His Paths?!"

"Look, these nations are those human beings who forever in the future will return to Me, and they will make My Word their own and do My Will; for My Word shows the road to life, and through the Word, My Proclaimed Will shows the path to the people. However, the strict observance of My Will is considerably more cumbersome than mere listening to My Word, as it is surely far more comfortable to walk on a broad and even road instead of on a narrow and often very steep path.

But whosoever wants to reach the highest of all mountains and there enter into My Living Word, which is the Lord's house on the mountain, must not only walk on the road which leads to the mountain and stop there, but he must also get onto the narrow and often very steep path; for only on this path does he finally reach the summit of the mountain and thereby the living House of God.

I have explained to you what this means, also what the prophet means by Z'e on and by Jerusalem; this is why he says that from Z'e on comes the law, and also My Will, and from Jerusalem, or from My Mouth, comes My Word.

Whosoever hears, accepts, and lives by My Word which I have spoken at all times to the people through the prophets, comes thereby to Me and also to the living word and its power, and everything that boundless space will hold is nothing but My Living Word and its eternal strength and power."

Thereupon one of those Pharisees who had come to Me on the Mount of Olives, and who was also a scribe, said: "Lord and Master, Your explanation of the two verses was as clear as the midday sun, and everything became very clear and obvious to me, but now comes the fourth verse which reads as follows:

'And the Lord will judge among the heathens, and will punish the nations. They will turn their swords into ploughs, and their spears into sickles; nations shall not lift a sword against nation, nor ever again be trained for war.'

Who are the nations and who are the heathens who, after having been punished, are no longer allowed to war against each other? These nations have yet to be born in a most distant future; for the present generations with their proud, greedy and tyrannical kings will wage wars until the end of the world."

Said I: "I admit you are a scribe, memorizing the law and all prophets well indeed, but you certainly did not ever understand them in the true spiritual sense! You have embarked on the wide and even road; but you have not put your foot onto the narrow path which leads to the mountain of true recognition.

Whosoever, through acting according to the law, does not reach the summit of the mountain of the Lord and enter into the House of the Lord, or reach to the inner living word from God, does not recognize the true, inner, living spirit of the law and the prophets."

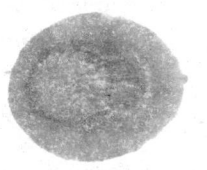

EXPLANATION OF THE FUTURE METAPHORS OF ISAIAH

Said the scribe: "But why have all prophets spoken and written in such a veiled manner? It should have mattered the greatest to them that their words be understood by the people!"

Said I: "Such objections were some days ago also uttered on the Mount of Olives, and I have shown you that they had no foundation, therefore I need not repeat here that which has been said before."

"What would a Word of God be if it had no inner meaning?! Or, can you imagine a human being without entrails? Learn to think truly wisely for once, all of you! But now I shall show you the so-obvious, true meaning of the fourth verse of Isaiah, so pay attention!"

"The Lord, which I am in the word, will judge amongst the heathens, and will punish many nations!"

"Who are the heathens, and who are the nations? The heathens are all those who do not know the one true God, but pray to and venerate in His place dead idols and the mammon of this world. Judaism is surrounded on all sides by this idolatry, and wherever you are in the world - may it be east, south, west or north - you will find only heathens of every kind and type. But you know that heathens of high and low standing and from far and near have come to Me from all directions. They heard My Word and saw My signs, began to believe, accepted My Teachings, and My Word judges and rectifies among them, whereby they cease to be heathens, changing over to the number of God's anointed and to the true nations of God.

But they also will not remain in the present faith; for soon there will arise false anointed men among them, working signs, bedazzling kings and princes, who will soon usurp great worldly power and persecute with fire and sword those who will oppose them; and in the end they will divide into many sects and parties. And precisely these are the many people whom I, as the Lord, shall punish because of their lack of love, their falsehood, selfishness, pride, stubbornness, lust for power and evil quarrelling, their persecution of each other, and warring. But until that will happen, quite some time will have elapsed, as has since the days of Noah up to now.

As it was at the time of Noah, when people married and gave in marriage, held great festivals and banquets, allowed themselves to be greatly honoured and made war against those who did not bow their knees before their idols, when soon the Great Flood came drowning all evildoers, thus it will be at that future time. But then the Lord will come with the fire of His zeal and His wrath, sweeping all these evildoers off the face of the earth.

Then it will come to pass that the spared, who are pure in heart and good, and the friends of truth and of the light from God, will turn their swords into ploughs and their spears into sickles, and completely abolish the art of warfare; and thereafter no truly anointed nation will lift up a sword against another, except for some heathens scattered about in the deserts of the earth; but these also will be reprimanded and then swept off the face of the earth.

Thusly will the earth be blessed anew. Its soil will bear a hundredfold fruit of everything, and the elders will be endowed with power over all the elements.

Behold the fourth verse in accordance to the spirit has to be understood as being the earth which you, as a scribe, considered to be incomprehensible.

But within this natural, true spiritual meaning is hidden a still more profound, purely spiritual and divine meaning which you cannot now grasp with your still-worldly reasoning, and such cannot be described with words. You will not walk in the true spiritual light of God until you will have entered the House of God on the mountain of the Lord and will then come from this house of Jacob, according to what the prophet says in the brief fifth verse. Tell Me if you can now understand this better than before."

EXEGESIS OF ISAIAH 2:6-22

[The Lord]: "And the prophet continues: 'Thou has abandoned Thy nation - the house of Jacob; for they are crowded with traitors and barbarians like the Philistines, and with the children of foreigners everywhere. Their land is filled with silver and gold, and there is no end to their treasures; their land is filled with horses, and there is no end to their chariots; their land is filled with idols, and they bow down to the work of their own hands, to what their fingers have made. The vulgar boweth down, and the great man humbeleth himself; and You Lord will not forgive them that. Go forth you unfaithful nation, enter into the rock, and hide thee in the dust, for fear of the Lord, and for the glory of His majesty!"

"These five verses belong in one category because they show the miserable state of the church or of the House of God on earth, with the Jews before this time, as well as with those who will come after us.

The reason I allow My nation to forsake the House of Jacob on the mountain of the Lord is because of their indolent way of practising God's Commandments and for the same reason, I also allow them to closely imitate the actions of the most barbarous and indolent nations who live in the Orient like wild animals.

And that which the Pharisees and the Jews of their kind are now doing, our descendants will also do: They will institute for the people a number of days to which they will attribute a special significance and effect, and those who will be against this, they will persecute with fire and sword. At the same time there will be soothsayers who will predict people's fortune and misfortune, allowing themselves to be exceedingly praised and well-paid; after all, such idle pursuit is more rewarding than wielding ploughs and sickles.

In order to increase their easily-earned income they will send, as the Pharisees do at present, their apostles out into the world to adopt the foreigners as their children. They were already good-for-nothing as sinister heathens; but after having embraced the true-world Philistinism, they will become a hundred times worse than before! Through which their sinister country will become one overflowing with gold and silver, and there will be no limit to their greed for the riches of this world, neither to their lust for power and passion for war, - which the prophet expresses metaphorically by an immense number of horses and chariots. Besides, the territory they rule will be full of idols and temples, such as was begun by Solomon the Wise in spite of the Lord's personal warning, who, on behalf of his foreign wives, erected temples around Jerusalem in honour of false deities. These blind fools will bow before such idols and pray before the work of their own hands and fingers, in the ridiculous belief to be pleasing God. And whosoever will not do this, will be persecuted in the flesh as a matter of life and death. And this because many kings will, for the sake of greater splendour of their throne, adhere to the nonsense of the World-Philistines and constantly pursue with fire and sword the ever so few friends of the light and of the living truth.

And behold, then the Lord will come and punish those nations who in His Name have bewitched so many people!

Then the true, living light will suddenly emerge from all sides and the friends of darkness will be conquered forever. Although they (the great and mighty of the earth) will flee to the mountains and hide in their barren soil for fear of the truth and majesty of the Lord, it will be of little avail to them."

Now the prophet continues with emphasis: "Man's high eyes (the pride of the rulers) shall be humbled, the loftiness of men brought low, and the Lord alone shall be exalted in those times and then eternally for ever and ever. The Lord Zebaoth's Day (Light) will pass over everything that is haughty and high and everything that is sublime before the world, so that it can be humbled; and it will also pass over all the cedars of Lebanon (priests), and over all the oaks in Bashan (the main supporters of the priesthood of idolatry for all times); over all the high mountains (rulers), and over all the lofty hills (noblemen of the king's court); over all high towers (the generals); and over all strong walls (armies); also, over all the ships on the oceans (those at the helm of government); and over all the earthly, exquisite labour (the great national industry). And, it will come to pass, that everyone must cringe to whatever is exalted among human beings, and all exalted human beings will be severely humbled, and only the Lord shall be exalted in those times. There will be no more idols in those days. Yes, in those days, man will enter the caves in the mountains and the crevices of the earth (mammon's hiding places), and that is done out of fear of the Lord and His Glorious Majesty (the Light of Eternal Truth) when He rises to inspire the earth with fear (punish). On that day, every man shall cast away his idols of silver and his idols of gold which he has made for himself to worship; he shall cast them into the mole-hole and into the caves of bats, so that it is easier for him to creep away into the crevices of rocks and cliffs, from the dread of the Lord and the splendour of His Majesty, when He rises to inspire the earth with fear! But it will be of no avail to anyone! Therefore, have nothing to do with such a human being who has any kind of breath in his nostrils (breath in the nostrils signifies worldly pride)! But you do not know how high his position in the world is!"

"Well, there you have the entire, easily comprehensible explanation of the entire and most remarkable second chapter of the prophet Isaiah! The latter verses are self-explanatory, provided one has grasped the significance of the first.

But I am telling you, it will truly come to pass now already in recent times and again to its fullest measure in approximately 1900 years; because even in My Counsel, there are no other means, since human beings must be left with their freedom of will, except for this one and only thing with which from time to time you can fruitfully face human indolence. It is the root of all sins and depravity. Have you understood all of this well? In regard to this, you will perhaps now sense less joy within you, but future nations will experience greater joy when they will be given these tidings anew in those times during their great tribulations, when one nation will rise against another for the purpose of corruption. But this shall be elucidated in the next chapter! Tell Me now how you have understood this so utterly important matter! I say 'utterly important' because I want to place it close to your hearts, as My future followers, to protect yourselves and all of your disciples from indolence."

EXEGESIS OF THE THIRD CHAPTER OF ISAIAH

Conditions in a well-ordered community

[The Lord]: "The following chapter also has a prophetic validity for now and for the times that I have proclaimed in the past.

Thus reads the very significant first verse of the prophet: 'Behold, the Lord, the Lord of Hosts doth take away from Jerusalem and from Judah the stay and the staff, the whole stay of bread, and the whole stay of water!'

Under the expression 'Jerusalem' understand here the present-day Jewry - as it is now and has been for a long time; but by 'Judah' understand the future generations which, through the acceptance of My Teachings, will be classed with the Jews. By reason of their great indolence, they can expect the same fate to a much greater extent than the present-day Jews can to a lesser extent.

By the taking away of the stay of bread is understood the taking away of love and mercy; and by the taking away of the stay of water, the taking away of the true wisdom from God; and as a consequence, all of them will be walking in great confusion and darkness of the soul, and no one can advise the other; and even if someone would advise another, the one in need of advice and light cannot trust the former but will say: 'How can you speak to me about the light, being in the same darkness as I!' The complete helplessness of the people, caused by their indolence due to their own fault, is rendered very aptly by the prophet in the following verses:

'Thus will be taken away the men of might; and the men of war, the judges, and the prophets, and the soothsayers, and the prudent, and the elders; counsellors, and the cunning artificers, and the eloquent orators, and the captains of fifty, and as well the honourable people.'

I deliberately place here the captains and the honourable people last instead of at the beginning of the third verse, for which there is a reason. And now understand this elucidation!"

"Who are the mighty and the men of war? They (the mighty) are men such as was David - full of faith and trust in

Me - and the men of war are those people who become inspired by the faith and trust of the one to such a degree as to conquer at any time over ever so many enemies of the goodness and truth from God."

"But who will be a true and just judge among men, once the living water from the heavens will be scarce among people, and all flesh, together with its souls will be in utter darkness? Who will then have the gift of prophesy? And even if somebody had it, who will believe him without inner reason?! Who will be able to prophesy to those who are blind and deaf in spirit?! And whom will sinister mankind, while groping in darkness, elect as a true elder and as their shepherd by virtue of his supreme wisdom?! Therefore, understand this matter well!"

"Whosoever has had bread and water in their spiritual significance taken from him, has had everything taken from him; for he whom God punishes and chastises with spiritual blindness is the one who is punished and disciplined the most. For everything has been taken from him, and he is completely devoid of counsel and help. But those are the ultimate means by which to effectively counteract the ever-increasing indolence of people and all their many depravities.

Through the taking away of the spiritual bread and water, human beings must truly find themselves in the greatest of misery, and in addition whatever else they are deprived of is further witnessed by the prophet in the third verse, where he emphatically declares: The people will also be deprived of their counsellors or advisers and the good artisans in all branches of human need, as also clever orators who previously used to work a great deal of good with their wisdom.

However, the worst of the matter is the simultaneous taking away of the, say, fifty captains! Who are these, and of what significance is the number fifty? The reason you will soon understand.

If we imagine a very large and perfectly-ordered society of human beings, and if this community wants to be well-provided for, since time immemorial it had to have in total, numerically speaking, fifty main branches to provide for and attend to the necessities of life. What is above that already belongs to pride, and what is below is already weakness, want and poverty. For every single branch of these essentials of life to be properly provided and handled, it must also have, as a supervisor and director, an able captain who knows his business from A to Z; should there be none, or one ignorant, this branch of human need of the whole community will soon begin to bear bad fruit or even no fruit at all.

How is a large community to exist after it has, through its indolence and negligence, finally become barren of all fifty captains? I tell you: exactly as it now exists in the large community of the Jews where only certain thieves and robbers still own property and live of the fat of the land at the expense of the poor, and only provide for their own bellies, while thousands helplessly starve in abject poverty. For where is the wise captain to take care of them by giving them work and food in one or the other branch of employment? Look, he is not there in many a branch, and therefore everything else is also missing! There are indeed still certain captains (leaders) to head the various branches, only not for the sake of the people, but for their own; therefore, they are nothing but thieves and robbers, not rightful captains as at the times of My Judges.

Now you have seen how the outer and inner welfare of the people of a large community is dependant upon the main leaders in the various branches of human necessities; but on whom does the proper appointment of the aforementioned captains in a large community depend upon in a country ruled by a sovereign or a king? Behold, just on one wise king!"

What does our prophet say: "What else will the Lord do to the indolent, godless communities?"

Listen, His Words are as follows: "I, speaketh the Lord, will give children to be their princes, and babes shall rule over them! And the people shall be oppressed, every one by another, and every one by his neighbour; the child shall behave himself proudly against the elders, and the base against the honourable!"

"The words of the prophet are in themselves so clear and true as not to need any further explanation; I can only draw your attention to the great and obviously evil consequences, although they are easy to find by themselves. Once in such a disorderly country all living conditions have deteriorated into the greatest of disorder, and all people of the community have fallen into great discontent because of their great want, then there will be one brutal uprising after another. The people will awaken, rise up and drive away or even kill the princes and selfish leaders. And this is where it is being said: 'One nation wages war against another.'

For as long as man, in his blindness, can fill his stomach with an ever-so-meagre meal, he bears all oppression owing to his indolent character; but should even this come to an end and only death by starvation looms before his eyes, he is sure to wake up and turn into a furious, hungry hyena. And this has to happen until mankind wakes up."

THE COLLAPSE OF
THE FALSE RELIGIOUS FRAMEWORK

Expounded from Isaiah 3:6-26, 4:1

[The Lord]: "Everything now is destroyed and slaughtered. Whosoever could be falsely accused, through his own merciless selfishness, of having contributed to the common misfortune of the nations will, unfortunately, fall victim to the revenge of the populace. But what then? The people have no leader left now, either good or bad. Total anarchy prevails, where in the end everybody can do as he pleases; but anyone who is mightier can also punish him to his heart's content!

Then those with more wisdom will come together, saying: 'That cannot continue or remain as it is! We, wiser and mightier ones, acquiescent to dispose the people to elect a wise leader with us. And it will be a great house, that two brothers of diverse, acknowledged experience will occupy!" What will happen then and there? The prophet shall truly tell us! And what does the prophet say?

Listen! He says: 'When a man shall take hold of his brother of the house of his father, saying: Thou hast clothing (knowledge and experience), be thou our ruler and let this ruin be under thy hand! In that day shall he swear, saying: I will not be a healer, for in my house is neither bread (belief and goodness) nor clothing (truth and faith); make me not a ruler of the people. For Jerusalem is ruined, and Judah (the later time) is fallen, because their tongue and their doings are against the Lord, to provoke the eyes of His Glory (the Light of His Wisdom). The shew of their countenance doth witness against them; and they declare their sin as Sodom - they hide it not. Woe unto their souls! For they have rewarded evil unto themselves!'

But the chosen sovereign, possibly I Myself, continues: 'Say ye to the righteous, that it shall be well with him; for they shall eat the fruit of their doings. Woe unto the wicked! It shall be ill with him: for the reward of his hands shall be given him. As for My People, children are their oppressors, and women rule over them. O My People, they which lead thee (false comforters) cause thee to err (see Rome!), and destroy the way of thy paths.'

The Lord standeth (in readiness), and He will then come forth to right the wrongs and judge the nations. The Lord will enter into judgment with the ancients of his people (the Scriptures), and the princes thereof (the awakened of recent times); for ye (Pharisees and Romans) have eaten up the vineyard; the spoil of the poor is in your houses.

'What mean ye that ye beat My People to pieces, and grind the faces of the poor?' saith the Lord God of Hosts.

Moreover the Lord saith: 'Because the daughters of Zion are haughty (the false teachings of the whore of Babel), and walk with stretched-forth necks and wanton eyes, walking (arrogantly) and mincing as they go (like a hungry dog), and making a tinkling with their feet: Therefore the Lord will smite, with a scab, the crown of the head of the daughters of Zion, and the Lord will discover their secret parts (take their reasoning away).

In that day the Lord will take away the bravery of their tinkling ornaments about their feet (those believing blindly), and their cauls (faithful followers), and their round tires like the moon (various orders), the chains, and the bracelets and the mufflers, the bonnets, and the ornaments of the legs (superstitious sectarianism), and the head-bands, and the tablets, and the earrings, the rings, and the nose-jewels, the changeable suits of apparel, and the mantels, and the wimples, and the crisping pins, the glasses, and the fine linen, and the hoods, and the vails (all of the glittering ceremony of the whore of Babel), and it shall come to pass that instead of sweet smell there shall be stink; and instead of a girdle a rent; and instead of well-set hair baldness (serpent-like cunning of the whore of Babel); and instead of a stomacher a girding of sackcloth; and burning instead of beauty.

Thy men shall fall by the sword, and thy mighty in the war; and her gates shall lament and mourn (because nobody will walk through them any more), and she being desolate shall sit upon the ground. And in that day (as there will be few men left because of the many wars), seven women shall take hold of one man (i.e. the seven sacraments will become only one) saying: we will eat our own bread and wear our own apparel, only let us be called by thy name, to take away our reproach!'"

Now look My friends: "That which the prophet has said will with certainty come to its fulfilment as I Myself have now explained it to you. For the people cannot bear the truth for any length of time; they truly tire and always fall back into their former judgment and death-inviting indolence and, truly, nothing else can then be done but to awaken the people through the most extreme means and to transpose them again from their former activity onto the ways and the Path of Light and Life.

Therefore, I am telling you once again: Above all, warn the people against spiritual indolence; for with it come all the evils of which the prophet has spoken, and I must, alas, allow them! Contemplate on this!"

THE NUMBER 666

[The Lord]: "I will give you a measure by which you and everyone else may know where he should stand with his self-love, with his love for his fellowman, and with his love of God.

Take the number 666 which - in its good or bad sense - depicts either a perfected human being or a perfected devil.

Divide man's love evenly into 666 parts. Of these give to God 600, to the fellowman 60, and to yourself 6, then you have the right proportions of a perfected human being. But if you choose to be a perfected devil, then give God 6, your fellowman 60, and yourself 600!"

THE REVELATION OF JOHN

Text: "And there appeared a great wonder in heaven; a woman clothed with the sun, and the moon under her feet, and upon her head a crown of twelve stars: And she being with child cried, travailing in birth, and pained to be delivered. And she brought forth a man child, who was to rule all nations with a rod of iron: and her child was caught up unto God, and to his throne."
Chapter 12, verses 1, 2, 5.

(Received through Jakob Lorber)

"Who is the "woman" appearing in heaven, clothed with the sun? The "woman" is the noble image of a human being without procreative power, but capable of procreation and conception. This woman therefore is a perfect image of man, thus no caricature or an immoderate human being.

My Teachings are like the woman which will certainly appear in the most perfect heaven, because My Teachings are in Me and come forth out of Me, as does the woman who is a perfect image of spiritual man, though within itself not capable of procreation; but through her, man will become receptive to all that is good in love, meaning receptive for the pure, heavenly love of God as the eternal spiritual life out of Me, that is, the "child" with which My Teachings will be fecundated in the heart of man.

It is true that we are speaking here only of My Pure Teachings as I do of a perfect, heavenly woman, not of a false doctrine or a female ape. It is totally natural that this perfect woman, or My Pure Teachings, surely is enveloped with the Sun, or with My Light of Lights, because she comes forth out of Myself!

This most perfect, heavenly woman, or My Purest Teachings, is only capable of receiving heavenly love out of Me. Hence, she kicks the moon with her feet as the unstable symbol of self-love, or world-love, as a totally opposite polarity to her pure, heavenly being. She is also adorned with twelve "stars", or with the Ten Commandments of Moses, and above that the Two Commandments of (Christian) Love, but by no means with the twelve apostles or with the twelve tribes of Israel, but, as I said, adorned with all twelve laws of Life Eternal.

The woman, or My active Teachings out of Me within man, will be or is already pregnant. With what? -- have you never heard of being born again?! Does it not say: 'Except a man be reborn of the spirit, he cannot enter into the Kingdom of God?!'

Behold: The child with whom the woman is pregnant is the pure love of God which, due to manifold self-denial, gives great pain to natural man, until such time when this heavenly love in the spirit of man matures within itself into the sublime rebirth to Life Eternal.

Do not imagine that the mere teachings and the depicted woman could become pregnant, but only the living, active teachings, if accepted into the belief of a human being. It is that depicted pregnant woman from where God's Love is being born as a new child, and that is the rebirth to Life Eternal.

However, the child is a boy! Why not a girl, consequently a woman in origin? Because in this love lies, and must lie, the original procreative power, as it is in man but not in woman.

This child, or the Love of God (i.e. Divine Love) in the spirit of man, born out of My Teachings, will then with an iron sceptre or with the most unbending power of God, restrain all nations, or all demands and sensual passions of the world. Through this - because of Me - the spirit of man and all his inclinations towards Me will come closer, and he will find bliss at My Throne, which is the true wisdom out of Me eternally!

Look, this is the very easily comprehensible meaning of these verses; thus only in this true light everything must be considered and understood."

EXPLANATION OF THE REVELATION OF JOHN

(Received through Gottfried Mayerhofer 1875)

"The Revelation of John is a portrayal of customs and morals of the entire time which came upon planet earth, dating from My Transition into the spiritual realm until the time of My Return. This Revelation has been explained, investigated, and expounded by many a man. And yet no one has found the proper key with which to unlock the books of this holy word or has been able to properly judge the events and periods of time, all of which had to come after My Return Home, as long as man, as a free being, was master of his own actions. Now, as we are almost at the end of the entire prophecy and most of it already has happened, I will explain to you this Revelation step by step. After that you may judge for yourselves how far removed from the real meaning everyone was who tried to fathom out by the letter of the word what can only be explained by analogy.

Until man comprehends the interpretation or the spiritual sense of the Words - which is called correspondence - it is in vain to grasp the innermost sense of My Words. Even the great number of new words which you have obtained up to now bear witness to this. For the more often you read them, the more spiritual they become compared to many earlier different interpretations, whereas now the content becomes clear to you. You have to start from the premise that I, as Supreme Spirit, can think and speak only spiritually. Likewise, that I clothe spiritual thoughts and ideas in words comprehensible to you in accordance with the capacity of the human mind. Therefore, this is by far not the last interpretation of these words - as you comprehend and read them.

Thus, I once let John write down this story by adapting My ideas to his power of comprehension. Had I spoken differently to him, he would not have understood Me, would have either misinterpreted My Words, or dared not to write them down for fear of becoming a victim of delusion.

Thus you find in this Revelation only symbolic pictures! You find the "Wrath of God", the "Plagues" and many other expressions which, in those times, were often used even by the prophets but were not meant to be understood literally. I, the God of Love, can exercise neither wrath, nor hatred, or take revenge, which is absolutely impossible, although I, as God, could - by means of sudden annihilation or through moral coercion - get everything immediately back into the proper order.

Should I be on fire over things I Myself have created thus and not otherwise? Should I perhaps call down curses upon creatures which - just because I created them as free beings - had to fail and to fall in order to be able to recognize the great divine attributes and their value through the contrary. How could you appreciate the light, knowing nothing of shadow or darkness? How could you value the beneficial power of warmth, knowing nothing of the cold? How could you comprehend the sublime virtue, morality, or moral feelings, unless their opposites existed? How could you understand the idea of spiritual progress, unless you knew the road downwards?

Behold, hence it follows that in all the Scriptures of the Old and New Testament many a thing is contained which is not meant to be as the letter indicates, but only according to the power of the understanding prevailing at the time; but they still forever contain the great nucleus of the spiritual. This is why the spirits in the highest beyond and even the angels' spirits themselves will find therein evermore sublime truths; the higher they themselves are, the greater their own spiritual insight will be. Thus all My Words are forever a rich source of spiritual wealth which will never become exhausted because I, as Infinite Spirit, can only think and speak infinitely and have recorded this through My servants. Now we shall take another step forward and begin with the first chapters of the Revelation.

These first chapters are concerned with the seven congregations existing after My Ascension which, as the first and best, were meant to serve as a basis for the preservation of My Religion or the exegesis and elucidation of the Jewish religious cult. They were meant to indicate how to change gradually from the formal and ceremonial, over to a spiritual cognition in order to restore the actual, true value to the basic truths recorded in the Jewish religion.

These congregations, which consisted only of a few elect, were as novices - apart from the persecution of those of a different faith - also exposed to the errors resulting from the misinterpretation of My Words. Therefore, the symbolic reference that the members of the various congregations should keep to their leaders who would, as stars or lights, show them the way to take; so that also the congregations (and individuals) in unison with their leaders, should themselves become "beacons" or guides for others who still walk in darkness.

The following chapters contain admonitions to the various congregations. As everywhere else there arose false prophets, over-zealous propagators, and all possible aberrations of the human heart, precisely because the meaning of My Words was understood in various ways by various people. Furthermore, these congregations had diverse relationships, partly among themselves, partly with those with whom they had to live, and thus were exposed to many temptations.

In these seven congregations you will find all possible conditions which are bound to prevail among freely thinking people: the ardent adherence to a doctrine of faith as well as the secession from the same, the ardent comprehending as well as the misunderstanding, and the vacillating between the spiritual and the worldly direction. Just as you yourselves, forming, as it were, a congregation, can experience that "neither cold nor warm" is applicable to you as it once was more than one-thousand years ago. Also, you will get into conflict with the world surrounding you, the more you adhere to My Teachings, and then your activities and conduct are contrary to those of the rest of the world. Thus it has been with the founding of every new religious sect which believed to be on a better path. Likewise, it is now with you, and it will also happen to many others who make My Words available for the benefit of the world.

Something else is significant with these first chapters, namely, that the very number seven is being mentioned as a spiritual symbol (seven stars, seven congregations, etc.).

In order to demonstrate the number seven more clearly

before your spiritual eye, I have to call your attention to the importance of examining all odd numbers more carefully, so that you will better understand their importance and in particular all uneven numbers such as three or seven.

Look, if you consider carefully the number seven or also the number three - judging in terms of symmetry - you must notice that with the number three, of the two (single) digits, one is on either side, and with the seven, three are on either side:

★ ★ ★ ★ ★ ★ ★

For harmony in the spiritual sense is only possible where there is a basis or a central point around which everything moves, on which it depends, and by which it is supported. Now, with the number three you always have to regard the middle digit as the central point on which the others relatively depend upon, having come forth through it, or achieved meaning through it. Likewise with the number seven, where three on either side are the forming, complementing and binding factors of the whole.

Take My Seven Attributes, and you will find Order in the middle; for without Order nothing can exist, and thus it is the fundamental pillar of all that is created, if it is to be maintained. You see, although Order came forth from Love, Wisdom, and Will, Order must be the basis of the former, as well as of the following attributes, i.e. the basis of Earnestness, Patience and Mercifulness.

Take the first three attributes: Love, Wisdom, and Will. There again - Wisdom, like Order, is the fundamental pillar of the former. And if you look at the last three, Patience is the main factor between Earnestness and Mercifulness. For if I created free beings like Myself, Patience must first of all be present to prevent Me from destroying My Own Works.

What I am demonstrating here to you about My Attributes, you can also learn from the Law of the Seven Colors and the Seven Notes of Music, which are also material correspondences of My Spiritual Attributes.

We shall now proceed to the next chapters. Just as the

Revelation presents magnificent portrayals of all phases of My religious Teachings, so also must the explanations show you how everything took place. How, soon, the Thousand-Year-Reign is to restore this harmony which once existed between Myself and My disciples, and which later on will be restored between Myself and all of mankind so that there will be only one shepherd and one fold.

The next chapter discusses a vision of John, showing him the Lord and Creator as Supreme Ruler of the Heavens. His contemporaries viewed the picture as they perceived it to be: sitting on a throne, surrounded by the elders and the highest who were adorned with golden crowns. Here you can see again that I, to be comprehensible, had to make use of John's intelligence. Thus, the number of the elders, twenty-four, is the number of the highest priests in Jerusalem where twenty-five, including the High Priest, represented the whole Council.

As for the four animals and the sea of glass, the animals themselves are embodied attributes of My Own Self: the lion as strength or omnipotence; the calf as a symbol of gentleness; the human being as spiritual potency; and the eagle as ruler of the universal ether. The fact that these animals are endowed with many eyes and have wings just like eagles, means the universal sovereignty over earth and heaven. But, the sea of glass represents omniscience, meaning: Before the Eye of God everything is transparent, and His gaze travels through the whole universe with the speed of an eagle. With the strength of a lion He rules all, with the gentleness of a calf He remedies all abuses, and with His Spirit, like a human being in His Image, He ennobles and spiritualizes everything, so that even that which is material may, at some future time, return back to the point from whence it once proceeded. And after all the powers of creation - consciously or unconsciously - bowed down before the Sovereign Lord, the elders, representing the great spiritual world in the beyond, also fell to their knees to offer due praise to the Creator.

Thus John was first of all shown in metaphorical analogy what the majesty of a god is, before he was able to comprehend Who the One was Who He bade descend to this little earth in order to save people from completely losing their spiritual dignity. This is the beginning of the great fermentation process which was spiritually initiated on this earth to establish in fact the purest teaching, worthy for the Lord, as a human Son of the Earth, through His greatest humiliation, to bestow anew the highest human dignity to the inhabitants of the earth.

That which is the course of time caused resistance to all of this, and the final result of it all is described by means of corresponding metaphors in the following chapters. As it actually happened when the Divine was first exalted by man, then debased, but finally - as victory of spirit over matter - will introduce a permanent reign of peace and tranquillity.

In the next chapter John is shown a scroll, inscribed inside and out, and sealed with seven seals. This means My only and true Teachings, which I gave to the people in two comprehensible Commandments. This proclamation, through the Son of Man as a "lamb" (symbol of innocence and suffering) is what is meant by "unsealing" the Book of Life sealed with My Seven Attributes, so that He should make it known to the whole of creation and particularly to the people on earth.

The first seal represents a picture of a white horse arising from a scroll as a symbol of My all-embracing love, crowned with all the other attributes, and with a bow to wound the most hardened hearts, so that some day all would resolve in love. Out of love the world was created, out of love I descended to earth, and it is out of love that My first corner-stone is to consist, which will establish My divine Teachings on earth, and which can never be overcome.

The second seal produced a red horse, a symbol of wisdom, or in human terms, of reason and the power of judgment, which wants to analyze everything critically. It will compare the divine heavenly teaching with the material existence, thereby exposing the differences. The result will, therefore, not be peace, but conflict, as human passions conflict with the principles of the soul of the spiritually-minded man, resulting in fanaticism on both sides - religious wars externally, and inner conflict of conscience - as a necessary consequence of two extremes opposing each other.

The third horse emerging was black, and its rider was

holding a pair of scales. It was the firm and just will which is determined to follow its final goal, undeterred by any obstacles. The will corresponds also to justice, which ponders the actions, the good ones bringing their own reward, and the bad their own punishment. Justice should prevail everywhere, both in matters of faith and in social life. I, as Christ, taught mankind to better understand the Teachings they had received. I taught them love and wisdom, which "allots" love its rightful measure. I taught them tolerance or justice towards all, and these three seals are therefore the key as to how My Teachings should spread if they are to bring about the ennoblement of the human race.

The fourth seal shows you a pale horse, that is, of nondescript color, neither cold nor warm or metaphorically, as it says there, death. For death does not signify the end, but only a transformation. Thus the color of the horse is like the Path during the Transformation brought about by My Teachings, which can be walked either upward or downward: upward to a higher spiritualization through its acceptance, and downward through the brutalization of the noblest attributes which I, as Creator, have placed in the human heart. This seal corresponds to order or the orderly course of all that is created.

This naturally leads to the interpretation of *the fifth seal* where the sacrifices are depicted metaphorically which, for the sake of My Teachings, are made materially on account of the passions of mankind. Already it is hinted what will be the reward of victory for him who sacrifices to the spiritual his utmost on earth - his own nature, and his own physical body. Thus where here metaphorically depicted previously as the scales of justice, the retribution and supreme bliss which come to those who, in the midst of strife, succeed in holding high and protecting the banner of their God and His Teachings.

The sixth seal shows you a total revolution on the whole earth, that is, correspondingly: The driving force towards the spiritual teachings will change all social conditions. The ardent haste to reach that goal will incite the opponents to equal haste. There will be war and destruction internally and externally; those in power will charge against weak nations, and the nations against their rulers, if their rights are curtailed too much. Thus the religion of love, peace and tolerance will, in the battle for its own survival, only give rise to the opposite, and these powers will war with one another until the spiritual will triumph. This sixth seal therefore corresponds to patience, which means nothing other than: It is in vain to strive against it! Where a god wants to impose his divine right, even the rocks have to give in, for his are justice and glory for ever and ever!"

And behold, those marked with the seal correspond to those who have overcome and who have been granted the bliss of which I once spoke: "Those who believe in My Word and act accordingly will enjoy everlasting bliss in the beyond, of which no human eye has ever seen or heard." This bliss has been indicated by the white raiment as the symbol of innocence. And those marked will receive the reward for all the sufferings and tribulations they have endured for My Sake and in the name of My Religion.

In this way the whole picture will gradually develop, clearly depicting the whole history of My Teachings during certain periods in time, from the first word of love to all religious wars, persecutions, and sacrifices by fanatical priests.

The opening of *the seventh seal*, or the end of the whole developmental process, when in spite of all plagues and tribulations, mercy finally does its work, is depicted by the seven calls of the trumpets and the ensuing plagues, which will only be a means of cleansing to lead people back to the ultimate good. The trumpet calls likewise depict the moral-spiritual changes which are taking place in the human heart as soon as the two-edged sword of doubt intervenes and the distrust of disbelief lashes its scourge.

Thus, the incense offering (sacrifice) on the altar of love was, metaphorically, a plague for selfish mankind. As, metaphorically speaking, everything withered away, so man in general closed his heart to all noble qualities; he wanted no part of a religion demanding sacrifices and curbing his worldly passions.

As fire, figuratively, destroys everything, so the selfish passions again destroyed all that was good. Persecutions replaced tolerance in matters of faith - one tried to destroy with blood that which was purely of a spiritual nature and therefore ineradicable. Thus it was still among the Romans in the early Christian times, when all possible atrocities arising from fanatical religious customs existed among the heathen priests, on which the latter imprinted the stamp of religious sanctity.

What happened to individuals was later extended upon the masses; the more the faithful grew in number, the more the persecutions grew against them; the greater the zeal for the pure teachings, the greater the sacrifice of martyrdom. Thus it happened after the fall of the Roman Empire that two bishops sat on the throne, one in Byzantium, the other in Rome. Never in agreement, they always nurtured this disharmony for their own advantage. As in earlier times, Christians were persecuted by the heathens, so now the popes persecuted the masses who did not believe what they thought was right, or what they chose to declare as truth at that moment.

It is from the time of the division of the Roman Empire, when later on the Bishop of Rome became Pope, that the religious wars began; the quarrels of the Church Councils, the persecutions by Church Inquisitions, the subjugation of the kings by the popes, and finally the Crusades. Then came the attempts for reformation and the bloody consequences of the latter in all countries, as also the development of various diseases such as the plague, etc., through the intermingling of the human races. All this is metaphorically represented by the trumpet calls and the vials of wrath, as also the corresponding spiritual metaphor "The Woman's Battle with the Dragon": a picture of the battle between human passions and worldly interests on the one hand, and spiritual progress and teachings of love on the other. Furthermore, the labour pains in leading the once-begun work to an end; likewise, the violent struggle which the Evil One incited against all who turned towards the spiritual.

All these allegories as seen by John are but expressions of the fierce resistance which My Teachings had to evoke, and its natural sequence when, in the war between good and evil, good must, and will, finally triumph. Do not take offence at the form of the allegories; they were in accordance with the comprehension of that time and with the manner of writing then in usage. In no other way was it possible to influence mankind for centuries to come, which knew little love and at the utmost, submitted only to fear. Had I, as God of Love, ordained the whole process of development up until now to be written in the language prevailing at the time, the words would have faded away, and nobody would have cared about their spiritual meaning.

The scorpions, the dragons with seven heads, ten horns and golden crowns signify the manifold exegesis of My Teachings, as it sometimes, supported by worldly authority, coerced people to adopt certain religious dogmas and ceremonies, all of which then gave rise to many religious sects.

The allegories show the historically well-known supremacy of the church along with the means by which it rose to power; and also how people in great numbers fell victim to the fanaticism of the Roman Church and her Inquisitions. The subsequent description of how the religious zeal gradually abates and worldly thinking seemingly triumphs, of how gold and silver are now more sought after than spiritual wealth, you can read in the following chapters: The victorious rise of wickedness under the cloak of religious cults, later through the discoveries of the sciences and the decline of the former, but also of any religiosity, and the transition to materialism. Thus in these allegories, the fall of the Roman Church is predicted, however, not as if I rejected her, but as she has brought about her own downfall, and must be rewarded according to her own actions.

The slain prophets point to the martyrdom of former times, when many a God-inspired man had to die at the stake. Not a century has gone by without My sending prophetic awakeners who were to prevent mankind from becoming completely lulled into a spiritual sleep.

The vials of wrath and their particular effects signify the epidemics and wars which mankind called forth, partly through their own unnatural mode of living, partly through committing mischievous atrocities. Even now, you can observe how the effects of egotism, materialism, unbridled passions, in general and individually, bring about misfortunes of all kinds: Misfortunes at sea and on land, misfortunes through natural catastrophes caused by mankind's poor handling of their own soil, suicides and murders in any form as the result of a lack of religious feeling, lack of faith in the existence of another world, and so on.

Consider all of this together and write it down in the picturesque language of the Orient as once did My disciple John, and you could add even more vials of wrath to the seven, describing equally horrible conditions.

Thus My Teachings went through all phases of which the human heart is capable, from purest piety to blatant disbelief and rejection of all that was given. You see it before you in metaphor, from the strict adherence of My Commandments, from the pedantic exegesis of My Words, to the total rejection of everything spiritual which is preached by a thousand voices in a visible and in an invisible nature. It was given in the form of an admonition and trumpet calls, which, however, due to non-observance were closely followed by action or punishment. Starting with the vials of wrath and their outpouring - as a symbol of what is evil and morally and physically unnatural must bring its own punishment - you see it all clearly before you: How My Seven Attributes urge on, little by little, to that which is best; how the free nature of man is contrary to it, how aberration after aberration, and error after error follow. How all efforts to eradicate My Words completely from the minds of mankind is in vain, and how even the worst yet must, and will, lead to the best.

This long-lasting conflict of the dragon with heaven, this persecution of the woman with her infant son Christ as Peace-Bringer - all of this you will now clearly grasp. And it will become obvious to you that after the long tug-of-war, there must follow a decision, when it will be determined who is the conqueror and who is the conquered! You are now approaching this time. It is presented by the metaphor of the Thousand-Year-Reign as the spiritual life of peace which will be awarded to those who are not marked with the sign of the beast, but with the mark of God.

Just as prior to My Descent, a spiritual war in mild form was on between the spiritual and the material, and as this process of separation had to lead to a final result after My

Ascension, thus shall now dawn a time of peace after this more than thousand-year conflict. Then people will begin to be human beings again, as I created them and want them to be, if they are to be called My Children. This will be the time of retribution, the time when the spiritual has conquered the material, when man, as a citizen of two worlds, will feel as much at home in the one as in the other, so that at long last My Words will be understood, and My former descent onto your earth appreciated in the whole light of its divine mission, and followed with love. This will be the time when the dragon will be slain and captured, and the Ten Commandments of Moses and My Own Two understood in their true meaning. In this time of peace and tranquillity, also the kingdom of spirits will be able to take their active part, so that those left behind, inspired by the example of the living human being, will advance more easily than was hitherto possible.

This time in the Revelation is under the title of "The Thousand-Year-Reign" or "The New Jerusalem". For Jerusalem was once the location where the Holy Ark of the Covenant was kept in the temple where the eternal flame burned, and where only psalms and incense on the sacrificial altar announced the purest divine service for IEOUA. This Jerusalem was defiled and desecrated by its own priests, and by My experiencing death there as a human being, instead of a blessing, heaped the curse unto itself; this Jerusalem, which had its downfall predicted by prophets and verified by Me, will spiritually descend to your earth again. It will come as in the splendour of its early time, bringing peace and tranquillity to all those who believe in the One Who once preached in this city, suffered, was crucified, and resurrected. This city, as a symbol of the first congregation of the Creator with His created beings, will descend with the palm of peace for all who, after conflict and suffering, have attained the status of kinship with God.

As the Jews once only knew one Jerusalem, that is how it will be - there will only be one church, one shepherd and one fold. The religious sects will disappear, and God the Creator and Lord, Who once walked upon your earth as a human being, will be recognized as such; what He was, what He is, and what He will be for eternity: Your Leader and the Father of All.

The community of the spirit world will be enhanced by the fact that I Myself will come in person visibly to My Children to comfort them and to prove to them that all I once said, what My Apostles wrote, and what John said in his Revelation, will be fulfilled. Once all spiritual and material wars have ceased, then everyone will easily understand Me and shall willingly fulfil My Commandments, which begin with the love of the fellowman, and end with the love of God.

But even this Thousand-Year-Reign will be followed by another epoch when man's animal nature will make one last effort, and the Fallen Great Spirit will claim his descendants. Alas! His efforts will be in vain, and he himself will be faced with the question: whether to proceed forward or backward, which will decide his future existence or non-existence!

All this is the true essence of the Revelation of John. Given metaphorically, but read with spiritual eyes and in the language of correspondences (or analogy), it will clearly show you how this little flower of love, planted by Me in the hearts of mankind, can never be uprooted. And how this nucleus of divine origin could never be exterminated, either in a spiritual or a material sense, despite all the plans on the part of those in power. Love, being the fundamental attribute of My Own "I", was the reason why I created the whole universe! How could this spark ever be lost or destroyed? In vain did they all shake this edifice, in vain did man try to misinterpret My Words. It all rebounded upon them and they had to harvest what they had sown. So now you see how all scientific and hair-splitting exegesis of the love-word of the Holy Scriptures gradually vanish like snow before the Sun of Truth.

The greater the resistance on one side, the more quickly the process develops on the other. Thus, as a final result, all this activity will merely further My Teachings, place them into a more proper light, and more and more prepare the ground for the transition to the Thousand-Year-Reign. Then the new Jerusalem, as the symbolic Temple of Peace, will restore the union between Myself, mankind and the spirit world, where neither trumpet calls nor vials of wrath will bring forth devastating effects, but where even your earth, the beings there, like the animal kingdom and plant kingdom, will assume the same type of love that the people will have within them. A whole generation of human beings, united by bonds of love, will help one another, where neither master nor servant, but the bond of brotherly and sisterly love will unite whole nations; where territorial boundaries will disappear and heads-of-state and popes no longer try to enslave - the former the physical, the latter the spiritual forces.

Led also inwardly by a rational religion, they will more readily listen to the whisperings of other spirits and even My Voice and believe it. Thus even the intercourse with the spirit world will have become a binding agent by which death with its horrors will be banned from this earth, and the other world presented to you exactly as it really is.

Thus you have here a far-reaching spiritual interpretation of the Revelation of John. Not, however, as the world expects it from Me, but in a manner that the world could understand, had it only just learnt to read with spiritual eyes. Metaphors remain metaphors, and each metaphor is based upon a thought which then seeks to express itself individually in forms. This is how you must understand the metaphors of the Apocalypse, not word for word, otherwise, you would never find the real reason, because too many contradictions would arise.

Furthermore, you must also come to accept that a different association of ideas and thoughts prevail in the spirit world than those prevailing with human beings living here and, therefore, visions such as those seen by John must have a character different from your now-adopted, well-ordered speech. Look, since the earliest times, thought expressed itself not in a language of words, but rather in a pictorial language; even the ancient Egyptians themselves wrote such signs upon their monuments.

In the Orient, pictorial language is still in use. This is a remnant of times long past when mankind was closer to its primordial source, and its way of expression too was closer to the spiritual world.

All these examples prove also that after transition into a

higher life, according to the level of spiritual progress, the speech and communication between spirits will be different than the slowly word, of which you often have to use many to express a single thought. As to My whole creation, what else but a pictorial language is it to all of you? And this it will remain until you are able to recognize the deeper spiritual "why" inherent in it; why all this is thus, and not otherwise, created. As you have a language of your own, just as I have Mine in visible nature, so do the spirits of higher regions have their language of communication which apparently sounds different from that which is really hidden therein. Therefore, it is a futile endeavour for your scholars to clothe in mundane words concepts of a spiritual nature. For this very reason My present Words which, in addition to being the interpretation of a great Revelation, are meant to lead you a step further into My Household.

I will leave it up to you to understand the peaceful metaphors of the Revelation, and only expound the more severe ones in which seemingly nothing prevails but God's wrath and inexorable retribution - in order that you may not fail to recognize also in these metaphors the God Who is purely love. The time is approaching when the spiritual wind, which is already manifesting itself, will blow more strongly; when you shall not, like reeds, bend hither and thither, but will soon be inclined to take the proper path which I have outlined for you. There will, as the Bible says metaphorically, arise false prophets. Mankind will cause much mischief with the purest Teachings, with spirit communication, indeed, with everything, to serve to satisfy his animalistic passions. And until the Kingdom of Peace will dawn, many a vial of wrath will be poured upon mankind by the people themselves, as the parties will spiritually and materially oppose one another in a more hostile manner, the more time presses on towards the end. Through this battle, the last vials of wrath will come to their fulfilment, after which there will follow depression, misery, and lamentation, after all resistance has been in vain. Some will, in despair, but others will consolingly await the end in resignation and with it the victory of the good cause.

Most of that which is depicted in the Revelation as

developmental crisis has expired, but the worst is yet to come. But have patience and trust in Me! You want to become, or be, My Children. Show yourselves worthy of this name, and the palm of victory, as foretold in the Revelation, will not fail you. Be prepared for everything! It is not I, but mankind's animalistic nature, their artificially created disbelief, their unruly lust for power and money that will help to fulfil these metaphors of the vials of wrath and trumpet calls.

Naturally, a purification process must set in before I Myself re-enter your earth. As during sultry weather, the thunderstorm cleanses the air by forcing all noxious vapours down to earth so that pure air can again blow, likewise in the spiritual purification process, as the resistance is strong, it must elicit powerful outbreaks, without which no equalization can take place. On your earth, every conflict will end by all parties recognizing their own unconsciousness and My Omnipotence against which any resistance is futile.

Therefore, accept this exegesis of the Revelation as a portrait depicting to you all phases through which a divine idea has to pass before it reaches its actual value. Let these visions serve as a parable to you of how much it takes until the good conquers and the evil declares itself as being conquered! As spiritual thinkers, take these visions as corresponding hints. For as John saw the course of Christianity spiritually, this is equally mirrored in the spiritual and material development of every human curriculum vitae.

Such conflicts, such trumpet calls and vials of wrath are discharged on ideas. Happy is he who, while taking the most bitter medicine, knows how to extract its healing properties! The spiritual purification and developmental process remains everywhere the same battle of the spiritual against the animal nature: Self-sacrifice of one's self, tolerance towards others. Therefore, let everyone examine his life, and he will in these visions of the Revelation find more or less depicted the story of his own life!"

★ ★ ★ ★ ★ ★ ★